OF WESTERN EUROPE
AGAINST ISRAEL

THE WAR OF WESTERN EUROPE
AGAINST ISRAEL

Published by Devora Publishing Company
Text Copyright © 2003 by Joseph Carmi

Cover and Book Design: Ruth Erez
Editor: Evan Fallenberg

ISBN: 1-930143-77-X

Email: sales@devorapublishing.com
Web Site: www.devorapublishing.com

Printed in Israel

THE WAR
OF WESTERN EUROPE
AGAINST ISRAEL

by
Joseph Carmi

DEVORA
PUBLISHING
JERUSALEM ◆ NEW YORK

CONTENTS

Both Europe and the United States have large and active Moslem communities devoted to their compatriots in the Middle East. Both, too, have visible Jewish communities. Yet according to the Anti-Defamation League, there has been no increase at all in anti-Jewish incidents during the past two years in the US, while in Europe such incidents are sharply on the rise.

This book takes a close look at the disturbing upswing in anti-Semitic violence in Europe by investigating European attitudes towards the State of Israel since its inception; by paying close attention to statements made by leading politicians and opinion-makers; and by following trends in European media.

I can only hope that readers of this book will include not only Jews and their friends interested in understanding a phenomenon of nearly incomprehensible proportions, but also Europeans willing to engage in difficult self-examination.

Joseph Carmi
Jerusalem, 2003

INTRODUCTION

During the second half of the Twentieth century, substantial efforts were made to conclude the signing of important economic and commercial agreements between the nations of Western Europe and Israel. Similar agreements developed over time in the fields of culture and science. At the same time, however, these achievements did not stem European doubts with regards to the very right to existence of the State of Israel. For example, Europeans overwhelmingly supported Arab claims that all Arabs who used to reside in Israel and left during the War of Independence be allowed to move into Israel, including their offspring of second, third and fourth generations. Such Arab insistence would obviously bring an Arab majority and the destruction of the Jewish State. The same can be said of the Europeans today, who demand that Israel not respond in kind to the slaughter of Jewish civilians.

Western European tactics do not include the Arab practice of sending assassins or suicide bombers to the villages and towns of Israel. Rather, the leaders of Western Europe continually condemn Israel's proactive policy of preventing future acts of violence. One can only conclude that these condemnations basically send the old familiar message to the Jews that says, in fact, that Jews are not entitled to defend themselves.

Therefore the question arises: why do the nations of Western Europe adopt policies that are life-threatening to the very existence of Israel? What possibly could be the justification for such a policy? Are the inhabitants of Western Europe deeply infected with hate for Israel? Might Arab oil be a decisive factor in their consideration? Perhaps the illusion that the extermination of the State of Israel will soften the hatred of hard core Moslems to Western culture or whatever it represents? Has the influence of the "peace camp" in Israel been so strong that it has tilted liberal intellectuals in Western Europe toward the Arabs?

It could be argued that charges made by the Israeli "peace camp" – of conquest and occupation, of dominating a foreign people, of stealing water from the Arabs – have influenced European intellectuals. Such claims may very well influence Western Europeans in adopting certain political positions. However, this does not explain the mixture of apathy and sympathy that greets Arab acts of terror against Israel. Nor does it explain the embracing and emboldening of the leaders who send the gunmen.

The countries of Western Europe have a reputation as civil, cultured and progress-minded. In fact, however, it was only after centuries of war and conflict that friendly and neighborly relations belatedly evolved. Thus, the Western European acceptance of Arab leaders like Yasser Arafat, whose forces regularly perpetrate acts of murder, is incomprehensible and inexplicable. A case in point is the June 2001 bombing of the Dolphinarium discotheque in Tel Aviv, where an Arab suicide bomber ignited his belt packed with deadly explosives, nails and screws and killed nearly thirty teenagers. Quite coincidentally, German Foreign Minister Yoshka Fisher was a guest in a nearby hotel and had the "privilege" of witnessing first-hand the destruction, death and maiming. Yet even this traumatic event did not hinder Western European countries, including Germany, from condemning Israel.

Recently Arab suicidal acts have been upgraded to expand their activities to North America.

On September 11, 2001, nineteen Arab Moslems of Osama bin Laden's group of Al-Qaida hijacked and piloted several American Airline Boeing jets, smashing them into the World Trade Center in New York City and killing approximately three thousand innocent human beings. Immediately following that disaster, pundits predicted that Western European countries would be more sensitive to the reality of continuous Arab suicide bombings in Israel and would realize that suicide bombers could very well infiltrate the heart of Europe just as easily. Nothing, however, has changed in that regard. In an interview on the Danish television program *Profile*, Foreign Minister Mogens Lykketoft warned: "If we want to prevent a massive terror struggle in the West we must put an end to the conflict in Palestine." His intent – forcing Israel to yield to Arab demands – was clear. In his view, a relationship exists between the bombing of the World Trade Center in America and the inability to reach a peaceful agreement between Israel and the Palestinians.

Since the start of the current Palestinian uprising, Europeans have been turning the heat on Israel more and more. For months, European pronouncements framed in harsh terms have decried "excessive" Israeli military operations. These reached a fevered pitch during "Operation Defensive Shield," which also prompted Europe to draw its last and most threatening card: an economic boycott against Israel.

Recently, the European Parliament narrowly voted in favor of suspending the 1955 EU Free Trade and Association agreements with Israel, which includes high level political dialogue, cooperation in several key areas and valuable trade worth billions of dollars. At stake is more than 42 percent of Israel's international trade volume, according to Foreign Ministry figures.

The resolution also notably expressed "full support" for "Israeli reservists refusing to serve in the 'occupied territories'." EU parliamentarians have floated other drastic anti-Israel measures, including the suspension of European cooperation with Israel in the areas of science and technology, and the canceling of agricultural trade liberalization talks.

Better to understand and confront this reality than to go on acting as if it were otherwise.

The Struggle for Independence

Desperate to pry open the doors of their National Homeland and rescue their surviving kinsmen from post-war Europe's displaced persons camps, Jewish organizations intensified their attacks on British personnel and installations in Palestine while Jewish refugee vessels challenged the Royal Navy's extensive blockade of the coast of Palestine. At a time of grim austerity in the home islands, the burden of maintaining order in the Holy Land was no longer bearable. Beyond the scores of its personnel killed and wounded at the hands of the Jewish guerrillas, Britain had been shamed before the world by the tatterdemalion flotilla of Jewish refugee vessels, and exposed to the endless harassment of U.S. President Harry Truman.

On February 19, 1947, Foreign Secretary Ernst Bevin informed the House of Commons that he was referring the fate of Britain's embroiled Palestine mandate to the United Nations. During the spring and summer of 1947, a United Nations Special Committee on Palestine studied the competing demands of Jews and Arabs, and on August 31 produced a majority report that recommended partitioning the country into separate Jewish and Arab states, with the Jerusalem area to be placed under United Nations administration. Foreign Secretary Bevin denounced partition as "manifestly unfair to the Arabs," and likely to inflame the entire Moslem world. "A British deal struck with the Zionists," he warned, "would be poor compensation for the loss of Arab goodwill."

On November 29, 1947, the UN General Assembly approved partition, effective May 15 of the following year. The British immediately declared that they would terminate their mandate in Palestine and would assume no responsibility for implementing the General Assembly resolution. Further, Whitehall froze currency deposits belonging to the Jewish Agency (acting as a quasi-government of the Jews in Palestine) and to private Jewish firms, banks, and other institutions that maintained accounts in London. The measure threatened to bankrupt the embryonic Jewish State at the outset. It also denied the Jews a concomitant opportunity to take over the facilities of railroads and postal services. Concurrently, Britain continued to sell weapons to Iraq and Trans-Jordan. Moreover, it barred the Jews from organizing an official militia or from gaining access to crucial defense installations. Iraq received detailed advanced notice of Britain's timetable for evacuating its police fortresses in Safed, Nabi Yusha, and Tsemah. All these stockades were immediately occupied by the Arabs. Similarly, the British deputy police commander in Jerusalem provided an advance schedule of military evacuation from several Jewish neighborhoods north of the city, with the same consequences of Arab occupation.

As the British mandate ended on May 14, the armies of five Arab nations, including the Arab Legion of Trans-Jordan, commanded by British officers and equipped with Britain's most modern weaponry and armor, attacked the newly proclaimed State of Israel. In less than two weeks the Legion had achieved its objective of occupying some three-quarters of the Holy Land, including the Old City of Jerusalem and its Jewish quarter.

By late May 1948, the Jews had weathered the initial Arab onslaught. Consolidating their armed forces, integrating new recruits and weapons, they threatened to launch a counterattack of their own against Jordanian-occupied eastern Palestine and Egyptian-occupied southern Palestine. Until then, ironically, the British ambassador to the United Nations, Sir Alexander Cadogan – with the help of Western Europe – had blocked all efforts in the Security Council to achieve a truce in the Holy Land. However, when the tide turned in Israel's favor and the Israeli army had the upper hand, Cadogan pressed the Security Council urgently for sanctions against the "Zionist aggressors."

Western Europe did not call for the condemnation of the Arab armies but clamped a strict embargo of any weapons sales to Israel in its worst hour of struggle for survival. The fortunes of war, meanwhile, shifted in Israel's favor. As the Egyptians sought to renew their offensive in the Negev, the Israelis launched a pulverizing campaign of their own that drove the last remaining Iraqi and Syrian units out of north-central Israel. "This is a complete disaster," lamented Hector MacNeil.

The Israelis were keenly aware that even a minimal foothold in the Negev Desert would preserve Britain's opportunity for surrogate bases in Israel territory. On October 14, 1948, therefore, they launched a major offensive against the Egyptian expeditionary force. Within a week they reached and captured Beersheva, "capital" of the Negev. Thirty-five thousand Egyptian troops now faced the possibility of entrapment.

On December 22, Israel launched its climactic offensive. On December 28, an Israeli armored column actually crossed the Egyptian frontier and began rolling into the Sinai Peninsula. The Egyptian people were appalled by this unimaginable turn of events. Indeed, by December, riots had erupted in the streets of Cairo and Alexandria, and Egyptian Prime Minister Mahmud Fahmi was assassinated by members of the Moslem Brotherhood.

Help came to Egypt from Britain. Under the terms of the 1936 Anglo-Egyptian treaty, Britain was obliged to assist Egypt against any attack by an outside party. Bevin was prepared to exploit the treaty to validate Britain's presence in Egypt. In fact, the Egyptians in recent years had been seeking to abrogate the treaty, for it prolonged Britain's control of the Suez Canal; but now in their desperation, they were ready to accept British military help on their behalf. In turn, Bevin's warning to the Israelis was terse and specific: Unless they obeyed the latest resolution of the Security Council, Britain would be forced to fulfill its treaty obligations to Egypt. Accordingly, on January 2, 1949, Israel ordered its troops to withdraw from the Sinai.

For several weeks RAF Spitfires had accompanied Egyptian air patrols over the Egyptian-Israeli frontier. On January 7, 1949, Israeli planes shot down five of these British fighters. Declaring that Israel had made "unprovoked aggressions" against Egyptian territory, Britain put a squadron of naval destroyers in the eastern Mediterranean on high alert, then rushed two British battalions from East Africa to the Suez Canal zone and advised British citizens in Israel to leave the country forthwith. In fact, the Foreign Office was interested in considerably more than Israeli withdrawal from Sinai: Britain hope to oblige Israel to relinquish the largest part of the Negev as well. Bevin now pressed on Washington, emphasizing the strategic advantages for the West if the British maintained de facto control of a desert land bridge from Egypt to Trans-Jordan. However, Harry Truman's patience with the British was exhausted. On January 10, the president summoned the British ambassador and coldly told him: "Your planes have no business over the battle area in Palestine." At this point Bevin finally stepped back from the brink.

Winston Churchill, as leader of the opposition, had been for weeks taking the government to task for rejecting Israel's legitimacy as a sovereign nation. "It has established a government which functioned effectively. They have a victorious army at their disposal and they have the support both of Soviet Russia and the United States." Churchill proclaimed: "Whether the Honorable Gentleman likes it or not, the coming into being of a Jewish State is an event in world history to be viewed in perspective, not of a generation or a century, but in the perspective of a thousand, two thousand, or even three thousand years."

Indeed, for months after May 15, 1948, Cadogan refused even to allude to Israel by name at the United Nations, referring instead to the new nation as "the Jewish authorities in Palestine." Britain had continued to detain Jewish male refugees whom earlier it had intercepted at sea en route to Palestine and interned in Cyprus. Only on January 18, 1949, did Bevin authorize their release. Eleven days afterward, the Labour cabinet announced de facto recognition of Israel. More than another year would pass before Britain, in April 1950, upgraded its recognition from de facto to de jure.

CHAPTER TWO

The Suez-Sinai War

By 1952, one hundred million tons of shipping passed through the Suez Canal annually, and of this tonnage, thirty five million was British. Through Suez, British troop ships foreshortened by half the Cape route to the Far East. Moreover the Canal Zone was of even greater value to the British as a military base than as a shortcut for maritime passage.

In 1952 a military cabal overthrew the Faruk monarchy and took power in Cairo. Its leader, and later the nation's president, Colonel Gamal Abd al-Nasser, had required less than a year to project himself as a champion of Arab unity throughout the Middle East. If the British military presence were removed from Suez, Egypt under Nasser would gain possession of a cornucopia of military installations and further tilt the military balance against Israel. Access to Britain's abandoned RAF bases would shorten by one hundred miles Egypt's bombing route to Israel, and thus provide Egyptian aircraft with an additional fifteen minutes flight time over Israeli targets.

In fact, Israel's worst fears were to be realized. On July 27, 1954, following years of intermittent and acrimonious negotiations, Egyptian and British diplomats at long last initiated a treaty outline that presented a near total victory for Egypt. By its provisions, Britain would withdraw from Suez altogether. The bulk of Suez installations would devolve into Egypt's hands.

Meanwhile, with the exchange of Anglo-Egypt ratifications on December 6, 1954, the first stage of Britain's evacuation began. The United Kingdom had left behind supplies valued at £80 million. As its final legacy to Nasser, Britain also left behind an open arena for potential military action eastward, across the Sinai Peninsula.

By the end of 1954, Britain's Middle East preoccupations were shifted to the threat of Nasser's escalating counter campaign against the Baghdad pact. Nasser then orchestrated an augmented Palestinian guerilla campaign of his own against the Jewish state, enjoying the leeway to begin shifting the launching base for these operations from Gaza to the long and porous Jordanian border with Israel. Heavy clashes between Israeli and Jordanian army units reduced Jordan's King Hussein to near panic. Swallowing his pride, the young monarch then ignored the strictures of the Nasserites in his cabinet and turned unreservedly to his British patron. The response on October 1 was affirmative.

On October 14, the counselor of Britain's embassy in Tel Aviv informed Israel's foreign minister, Golda Meir, that his government "stood ready" to honor its treaty obligations with Jordan, and was "inviting" Iraqi troop units to protect key Jordanian security installations. Mrs. Meir did not flinch. "My government would reserve freedom of action," she told the British official. The RAF commander of forces in the Middle East recommended shifting a wing of Venom fighters from

British bases in Germany to Cyprus, and assigning Cambera bombers already deployed in Malta "for offensive action against Israel."

Late in the evening of October 14, 1956, Prime Minister Antony Eden issued orders canceling the planned transfer of Iraqi units to Jordan. The military scenario against Israel was similarly dropped. Eden was prepared at last to reappraise his government's approach to the small Zionist republic. Now finally with a much larger Egyptian danger looming on the horizon, no further provocations of the Israelis were to be risked, no further scenarios devised of returning to Palestine through a Jordanian back door. However belated, Britain's farewell to the Holy Land had by then become irreversible.

By January 1956 the last contingents of British troops had evacuated Egypt. On July 25, the Egyptian president dropped a bombshell: Inviting the Americans to "go choke on your fury," he announced his intention to nationalize the Suez Canal company, and to apply its future revenues to construction of the Aswan Dam. That night delirium reigned throughout Egypt. In his own country Nasser was hailed as a national hero, and in the Arab world at large, as a hero of anti-colonialism. London and Paris were stunned. The British government owned the largest block of stock in the Suez Canal Company, and private French investors owned much of the rest. Nearly a quarter of British imports passed through the canal.

On August 5, a joint team of British and French staff officers established a combined headquarters in Cyprus and set to work preparing a strategy for invading Egypt and seizing control of the Suez Canal. The impending operation, dubbed Musketeer, envisaged a combined naval armada of British and French warships, and British and French air units. The actual invasion force would encompass British and French troops. However, Washington's horrified opposition played a role. The allies, rethinking their invasion strategy, abandoned their plan for driving on to Alexandria and Cairo. Instead, the objective would be shifted exclusively to the Suez Canal area. This alteration, in turn, now provided the opening of collaboration with Israel. Thereupon Bourge's-Maunoury asked the most crucial question: In principle, would the Israeli government be willing to take part in the Anglo-French military operation against Egypt? In principle, Shimon Peres thought that it would. As riots in Poland lately had drawn the Kremlin's attention away from the Middle East toward Eastern Europe, and America's attention was largely focused on its presidential elections, Israel, being interested in sharing in an early offensive, thought that it could give a qualified yes.

Meanwhile, the Israelis and French reached an understanding. On October 23, French Foreign Minister Pineau flew to England and pressed the full scenario on Eden and Selwin Lloyd. For Eden the priority was to achieve Nasser's downfall, and the Franco-Israeli formula appeared likely to achieve that objective. On the spot, then, and over Lloyd's lingering reservations, he accepted all of Israeli demands. Ben Gurion insisted on formulizing the tripartite understanding in writing. The request was approved.

Only on October 26 was British headquarters in Cyprus informed that Operation Cordage, the blueprint for RAF attacks on Israel, was to be scrapped in favor of Operation Musketeer. It was then, too, that General Keightley, the allied commander, learned of the impending Israeli connection. (Stunned, Keightley muttered in disbelief to his adjutant: "They are bringing in the hook-nosed boys.")

Finally, at 7:00 p.m. on October 31, the allies launched their bombardment of Egypt's principal air bases. Late as it was, the air attack was effective. Pounding ahead swiftly, Israel's armored columns invested Egypt's key bases in central Sinai and in Gaza. By November 2, the Sinai was an open door for the Israeli army driving westward along the coastal road toward Suez. On November 4, the Egyptian garrison in Sharm al Sheikh surrendered. The Sinai war was over.

In New York, the UN Security Council met in emergency session on October 31 to condemn Israel's move into Sinai and to demand an immediate withdrawal of Israeli forces. For the first time in the history of the world body, Britain and France both cast vetoes. On the following day the General Assembly was summoned to circumvent the allied vetoes in the Security Council. US Secretary of State Dulles asked for a resolution condemning Britain, France, and Israel alike and demanding immediate Israeli withdrawal and the cessation of allied bombardment. The resolution was carried next day by sixty four votes to five, with only Australia and New Zealand joining Britain, France, and Israel in opposing it. On the night of November 3, with his nation's strategic objective all but fulfilled, Israel's ambassador Abba Eban informed the UN General Assembly that his government was accepting the cease-fire. On November 6, London too announced that it was accepting the United Nations' demand for a cease-fire; the accumulation of pressure, both domestic and international, had shaken Eden's commitment to Operation Musketeer. Yet it was not domestic condemnations alone that cracked Eden's resolve. On November

6, Washington informed the prime minister that Britain's impending one billion dollar loan from the International Monetary Fund was contingent upon a cease-fire. A sick man by then, Eden became completely unnerved. Frustrated and bitter, France's Mollet in the end was obliged to act jointly with the British. Operation Musketeer would end at midnight, November 6, and within the month, Eden would resign as prime minister. In reaching their decision, the British and French took note also of a warning from Moscow.

Ultimately it was the confluence of military, diplomatic and economic dangers that registered on Eden, and in lesser degree on Mollet, that impelled them to abort their painstakingly contrived Operation Musketeer. On the other hand, Israel had accomplished its long-held strategic objective. The blockade of the Strait of Tiran was broken. So was the back of the Egyptian army in Sinai. Gaza would no longer be a launching ground for terrorists; on November 4 the General Assembly approved dispatch of a UN Emergency Force (UNEF) to serve as a buffer zone between Egypt and Israel.

Among the Great Powers, France remained Israel's single dependable ally, both publicly and privately. Mollet, Pineau and their colleagues were unshakable in their loyalty. But on December 22, the last French and British soldiers finally departed Port Said. With the Suez phase of the episode over, Israel alone now confronted the heaviest weight of international pressure.

During the ensuing four months, the Jewish State waged a stubborn diplomatic campaign to avoid unconditional withdrawal to the 1949 Rhodes Armistice lines. The European delegations supported a series of UN General Assembly resolutions for prompt and unconditional Israeli evacuation.

Washington fully endorsed these demands. By then, the Eisenhower administration scarcely disguised its threat to impose economic sanctions on Israel.

The French monitored Israel's situation with intense solicitude. In late January 1957 Foreign Minister Pineau warned UN Secretary General that "France would not recognize any General Assembly resolution imposing sanctions on Israel. The French government is determined to provide Israel with all the help needed to meet her just demands."

Within the next few days it became clear that there existed a General Assembly consensus, rather than a formal resolution, for sending UNEF contingents to Gaza and Sharm al Sheikh. The Secretary General confirmed on February 26, 1957, in a memorandum, which Dulles endorsed in writing, that any future proposal to evacuate the UNEF must first be submitted to the General Assembly.

On March 4, the Israeli government began evacuating its troops from Gaza and Sharm el Sheikh, to be replaced immediately by six UNEF battalions. Nasser after all had emerged from his battlefield disaster with his prestige reasonably intact. He had camouflaged the brutal shellacking his army had suffered at Israel's hands under the palpable evidence of Anglo-French bombardment.

Meanwhile, terrorist infiltration from Gaza ended. Israelis in their nation's outlying border towns could now work and sleep in peace for the first time in nearly a decade. The Gulf of Aqaba was open, and Israel's freedom of passage there would remain unchallenged until May 1967.

Upon coming to power in 1958, General de Gaulle was approached by Jacques Soustelle, former governor-general of Algeria, who proposed a Franco-Israeli alliance. The president's cool response was: "Matters are fine as they are." Conceivably de Gaulle was expressing the view of his foreign minister Maurice Couve de Murville, a former ambassador to Egypt, who strongly favored a restoration of France's ties with the Arab world. Couve de Murville was moving discreetly to uncouple France from its intimate embrace of "gallant little Israel;" upon assuming his portfolio at the Foreign Ministry, one of his first acts was to replace the ardently pro-Zionist Pierre Gilbert as ambassador to Israel. From 1959 on, de Gaulle rejected any further suggestions of developing a joint Red Sea strategy with Israel. In the UN General Assembly, France's delegation refused to support a 1961 African initiative calling for direct negotiations between Arabs and Israelis. In August 1960, Couve de Murville shocked Israel's ambassador by declaring that France would no longer provide Israel with uranium for Israel's nuclear reactor, and also by requesting that the Dimona facility be placed under international supervision. By then the American U-2 surveillance and additional CIA investigation had confirmed the existence of the nuclear project, and Washington was pressing France and Israel to open the reactor to international controls. De Gaulle himself would have preferred that the cooperative enterprise be discontinued altogether.

In the summer of 1964, de Gaulle tendered a warm reception to Prime Minister Levi Eshkol, Ben Gurion's successor. The president offered a toast to "Israel, our friend and ally," then fortified his earlier commitment on the Mirage fighters with a pledge to sell Israel a squadron of Super-French helicopters. It would be the French president's last public gesture of friendship to the Jewish State.

CHAPTER THREE

The Six Day War

As the price for the humiliating defeat of their state clients, Egypt and Syria, the Russians in ensuing years felt obliged to offer Nasser rather more tangible compensation. It took the form of five hundred new combat aircraft, twelve hundred tanks, and fifteen hundred artillery pieces, as well as vast quantities of support vehicles and ammunition. The deliveries were in quality as in quantity. The re-supply effort was paralleled by equally substantial shipments of military hardware to the new Leftist regime in Syria.

The deteriorating Syrian-Israeli border situation was already electric with danger. Palestinian terrorists were crossing the frontier into Israel with greater frequency, each time accompanied by larger numbers of Syrian regular army troops. On May 15, 1967, Nasser dispatched two armored divisions across the Suez Canal and into western Sinai. Once these troops were in place, the Egyptian president – in a move that astounded the Soviets no less than the rest of the world – ordered the withdrawal of the 3,400-man UNEF force patrolling the Gaza-Israeli frontier, and the complete UNEF evacuation from Gaza.

On May 21, Nasser issued a chilling announcement: "The Strait of Tiran is part of our territorial waters. No Israeli ship will ever navigate it again." The Western powers failed to reach agreement on an international naval force capable of guaranteeing passage through the Strait of Tiran. The Russians manifestly had a vested interest in blocking the scheme. De Gaulle was opposed to any proposal not based on a Four-Power conference. Only Australia, New Zealand, and the Netherlands expressed willingness to commit naval vessels and risk Arab criticism. Israel stood alone, and actually vulnerable to Egyptian and Syrian forces vastly replenished by Moscow. Other Arab countries were adding their weight to Egyptian and Syrian combat strength. All diplomatic efforts by then had failed to lift the Egyptian blockade.

On May 20, 1967, Hafez Assad, who was then serving as Syria's defense minister, said, "Our forces are now entirely ready to initiate the act of liberation itself, and to explode the Zionist presence in the Arab homeland. I, as a military man, believe that the time has come to enter into a battle of annihilation." On May 26, Nasser declared in a speech to his nation, "Our basic aim will be to destroy Israel." On May 30, Cairo radio was even more explicit: "Israel has two choices, both of which are drenched with Israel's blood: Either it will be strangled by the Arab military and economic siege, or it will be killed by the bullets of the Arab armies surrounding it from the south, from the north and from the east." A week later the war began.

At 7:10 A.M. on June 5, the Israeli Air Force launched a preemptive attack on Egyptian air bases. Within the space of three hours, Israel's pilots had smashed the best equipped of these bases and turned three hundred of Nasser's three hundred and forty combat planes into flaming wrecks. The Israelis were free now to concentrate on a land offensive. This began the same morning. Two and a half days later all of the Sinai was in Israel's hands.

In a critical miscalculation, Jordan's King Hussein authorized his army to move in Jerusalem's demilitarized zone and began shelling the Jewish sectors of the city. Units of the Israeli army seized control of the Jerusalem mountain ridge, then swooped down on the rest of the Palestinian West Bank, easily overrunning its principal towns, including the Arab Old City of Jerusalem, with its ancient Jewish quarter, and Western Wall. On June 6, a Syrian armored infantry company launched a series of attacks on the Israeli frontier communities. The government issued the order to move against Syria. The task was formidable. The Golan Heights, from which the Syrians had rained their artillery shells on Israel's northern farm villages, was a perpendicular dragon's nest of impregnable fortifications. At high noon on June 9, the Israelis set out to ascend the Heights. The struggle was an inferno. But after a day of close-quarter fighting, the Israelis succeeded in ensconcing themselves on the Golan plateau. By the afternoon of June 10, their armored units had cracked the main Syrian fortifications. Thus, in less than six days, the entire Arab chain was in ruins. Israel's triumph was complete.

On the first day of the war, the Arabs claimed to have bombed Tel Aviv and destroyed Haifa. Nasser, continually mounting his own venomous propaganda, fell into the trap set for all liars, coming to believe his own lies. He sold his lies to King Hussein of Jordan and the Syrians.

More importantly, even the Soviets initially believed him. By the time the Arab debacle became apparent, the war was already lost, no matter what propaganda lies were still being advanced by the Arabs.

Consequently, the American position of 1967 contrasted vividly with the adversarial stance Washington had adopted after the 1956 Suez-Sinai war, when Eisenhower and Dulles had demanded unconditional Israeli withdrawal from occupied territory.

Britain

Addressing the UN General Assembly on June 21, British Foreign Secretary Brown maintained his opposition to unilateral Israeli withdrawal, but added the reproof that no nation should be permitted to secure "territorial aggrandizement" by war. On November 18, Lord Caradon, Britain's ambassador to the Security Council, presented a draft resolution that included the stipulation of "non-admissibility of the acquisition of territory by force," as well as a clause mandating "withdrawal of Israeli armed forces from territories occupied in the recent conflict." Yet the draft linked these demands with "termination of all claims or states of belligerency, and respect for and acknowledgement of the sovereignty of, territorial integrity, and political independence of every state in the Middle East, and their right to live in peace within secured and recognized boundaries free from threats or acts of force." When the Indian and Arab delegations, almost at the last moment, pressed for a clause demanding evacuation of "the territories," Caradon refused to include the definite article. On November 22 the Security Council approved the draft as Resolution 242.

However, under the Conservative government of Edward Heath, Britain resumed its traditional sensitivity to Arab oil resources and financial power.

France

The French position held that each of the Middle Eastern states had the right to exist, but none had the right to initiate hostilities; only a meeting of the four Great Powers could resolve the problem of navigation in the Gulf of Aqaba as well as the problem of "the Arab refugees." In Washington, President Lyndon Johnson's reaction to the four-Power proposal was a mock query: "Which are the other two?"

That same afternoon, June 2, de Gaulle ordered an immediate cessation of French weapons shipments and put a stop to deliveries of the Mirage aircraft and its spare parts to Israel. However, public opinion remained overwhelmingly sympathetic to Israel. On June 5 another mass rally took place outside the Israeli embassy, this one comprising some hundred thousand people. That day too, three Gaullist deputies departed for Israel, with other non-Gaullist deputies, to demonstrate their solidarity with the Jewish State.

Nonetheless, de Gaulle remained obdurate in his refusal to accept Israel's conquests as a fait accompli. On June 19 he explained to Harry Wilson, "France must align itself with the Arabs. It has vital interests with the tens of millions of Arabs."

Holland and Germany

Dutch support for Israel was intense and overwhelming. Prayer services for Israel's welfare were conducted in every

Dutch church, Catholic and Protestant alike. And once the magnitude of Israel's triumph became evident, the nation practically exploded in public relief and joy. In the aftermath of the Six Day War, the Netherlands and West Germany led the campaign for wider Israeli access to the Common Market.

German public concern for the Jewish State was overflowing. Three days before the war, the nation's most prominent citizens signed a petition urging "all who have public responsibility in our state not to stand silently aside but to stand by the Israeli people, morally, and by peaceful means." The full text of the appeal was carried gratis in most of the Federal Republic's leading newspapers. Torchlight demonstrations in support of Israel were conducted in all the larger cities. Ecumenical prayer services were held for Israel in Germany's Catholic and Protestant churches alike. On June 5, too, the Trade Union Federation decided to invest DM 3,000,000 in Israel bonds as a "visible expression of solidarity," and asked its members to engage in demonstrations "to reestablish the state of peace and to safeguard the existence of Israel." The Berlin Senate donated DM 30,000. Innumerable other collections and contributions were dispatched by private organizations and even by private individuals. In Bonn some one thousand doctors and nurses volunteered their services to the Israeli embassy for work in Israel.

But the euphoria of pro-Israel feeling could not be sustained and it turned to harsh criticism and condemnation.

After the Six Day War, the Dutch expressed growing concern at Israel's settlements in Arab-inhabited territory. Foreign Minister Josef Luns favored developing EC emphasis on Palestinian "rights" as an indispensable element of any peace settlement. In January 1971, Luns criticized *all* parties to the Middle East conflict for "not wanting to make concessions." Foreign Minister Pa Harmel of Belgium and Italy's Prime Minister Aldo Moro repeatedly entreated Israel to "give up all expansionist plans."

By May 1971, the EC had achieved enough of a consensus to issue its first *pronunciamento* on foreign affairs. Known as the Schumann Paper (after its author, French Foreign Minister Maurice Schumann), the statement recommended a progressive Israeli withdrawal from the territories, with only minor border changes, and free choice for Arab refugees either to return to their homes or to accept repatriation and indemnification.

Thus, in a short span of years following Israel's miraculous 1967 victory and the subsequent euphoria, European support for Israel vis-á-vis her Arab neighbors had all but disappeared entirely, and once again the fledgling nation was isolated and shunned.

CHAPTER FOUR

The Yom Kippur War

Y om Kippur is the holiest of holy days in the Jewish calendar. It is a day of introspection, a day of forgiveness, a day of atonement. No shops or restaurants or bars are open in Israel on that day. The media is silent until sunset, when the day of fasting and abstention ends. That was the day – October 6, 1973 – the Arabs chose to launch their attack on Israel, Egypt from the south and Syria from the north (Jordan had learned a lesson in bitter defeat in 1967 and abstained this time around).

Israeli intelligence, as well as the Israeli political and military echelons, were still basking in the 1967 victory and preferred to ignore the Egyptian and Syrian military concentrations on Israel's borders. By contrast, Anwar al Sadat's objective was exclusively one of military confrontation. To that end the Egyptian president anticipated the military cooperation of Syria. In 1969, the Syrian Jadid regime was overthrown by an air force colonel, Hafez al Assad. It was under his aegis that the Syrians became more thoroughly equipped for a military offensive than ever before in their history. Indeed, Sadat's eviction of Soviet advisers from Egypt had actually strengthened Assad's bargaining leverage with Moscow. To protect this Middle Eastern bridgehead, the Soviets agreed to ship Syria unprecedented quantities of military equipment, including three hundred new tanks, three hundred jet fighters, and five hundred late model SAM6s. Thus when Sadat proposed a joint offensive against Israel, Assad felt strong enough to respond favorably.

In July 1973, Moscow began shipping selective quantities of modern equipment to both Egypt and Syria. The weaponry included hardware as sophisticated as Scud surface-to-surface missiles and MiG 23 aircraft.

The war commenced in the north, with thousands of shells exploding along the Golan Heights. Soon, five Syrian divisions began rumbling along the cease-fire line, cracking the Israeli front in two sectors.

In the south, a firestorm of shells simultaneously descended along the eastern embankment of the Suez Canal. When the Egyptian barrage reached its crescendo at 2:25 p.m., Egyptian infantry moved across the waterway in fiberglass boats. Responding, Israeli jets were hurled against these amphibious forces, only to be shot down in large numbers by SAM6 missile salvos and other anti-aircraft weaponry. By midnight, thirty thousand Egyptian infantrymen had secured a beachhead throughout the eastern length of the canal, and had begun pushing through the Sinai. As Israeli tanks rushed forward, Egyptian troops lying in ambush fired off portable Sager rockets scouring Israel's armor, wiping out entire tank crews with each blast. By early afternoon of October 7, eleven pontoon bridges spanned the canal and three hundred Egyptian tanks and five mixed-infantry and armored divisions had crossed the waterway.

Meanwhile, the Soviets had committed their extensive logistical resources to support of the Arab offensive. Relays of East European vessels unloaded thousands of tons of weapons at the ports of Egypt and Syria. From Hungarian air bases, a continued relay of Antonov transport planes ferried guns, tanks, and dismantled jet fighters to Syria and Egypt.

On the first two days of the Arab offensive, Israel's outnumbered brigades on the Golan Heights waged a desperate rear-guard battle against a Syrian offensive that threatened to inundate the entirety of northeastern Israel. By dawn of October 9, however, additional tank reinforcements reached the Golan, and the Israelis launched a counterattack. During the next thirty-six hours their armor drove the Syrians well beyond the original 1967 cease fire line, and even to within twenty-five miles of Damascus.

By October 11, Israel's General Staff was able to shift its efforts to the Sinai theater. At dawn on October 14, the Egyptians hurled their full strength eastward; the effort proved disastrous. The Israelis destroyed some two hundred and fifty tanks and established full control of the field. Within hours, then, the Israeli General Staff turned to the offensive, preparing to counter attack across the Suez Canal. By the afternoon of October 17, two armored divisions of three hundred tanks and fifteen thousand troops crossed over the canal. Subsequently, Israel's invasion force fanned out on the western embankment of the canal. The Egyptian military situation had deteriorated. Israel stood on the threshold of total victory. At midnight on October 23, informed of the ominous developments, Sadat lodged a panic-stricken appeal for Soviet intercession. Washington and Moscow together devised a formula under which a Red Cross convoy would be allowed to bring medical and food supplies through Israeli lines to the besieged Egyptians. It was clear by then that hostilities would not be resumed. The most brutal of the four conflicts between Egypt and Israel had ended.

By early November 1973, Egyptian and Israeli negotiators at kilometer 101 reached agreement on a permanent supply corridor for the Egyptian Third Army, and on a full exchange of prisoners. In this fashion, the Egyptian president agreed to set about clearing the Suez Canal and rebuilding the canal cities. Nonmilitary cargoes to and from Israel would be allowed passage through the canal, although not in Israeli vessels.

By the spring of 1974, moreover, even Syria's President Assad was prepared to accept American mediation. On May 31, an agreement was reached for the Syrian-Israeli front, establishing a new and binding cease-fire, a minimal withdrawal of Israeli forces on the Golan Heights and a demilitarized buffer zone to separate the two armies.

For Sadat, intent on moving his nation's economy off its chronic war footing, the United States connection offered nothing less than a lifeline. On March 14, 1976, he asked his People's Assembly to cancel the 1971 Soviet-Egyptian treaty of friendship and cooperation. The request was immediately approved. In November 1977 Sadat revealed his own, dramatically simple, alternative route to peace. It would run not through Geneva but through Jerusalem.

The Western Europe nations did not condemn the Arabs for their attack on Israel. Instead they took a stand condemning Israel, rewarding the Arabs by denying American planes en route to Israel with supplies and munitions the right to land in European airfields.

In France the Pompidou government's pro-Arab bias was defined by Foreign Minister Jobert's caustic observation: "Can you call it unexpected aggression for someone to try to repossess his own land?"

In Britain the reaction of the Heath cabinet was even more shocking to the Israelis, for it produced an immediate suspension of arms supplies. Israel's main battle tank was the British-manufactured Centurion, and the embargo blocked all further deliveries of this armor, including spare parts contracted and paid for. More painful yet, London denied American planes access to landing and refueling facilities at RAF bases in Cyprus.

In supplying emergency shipments of weaponry, the US had intended to draw upon the equipment stored in its complex of NATO bases in Germany. Determined to avoid jeopardizing ties with the Arab governments, the West German government refused use of its airfields for the American re-supply effort to Israel.

When the Arabs launched their Yom Kippur offensive, the Dutch rallied again in support of the Jews. On October 9, 1973, their government officially condemned the Arab resort to violence and called for the return of Egyptian and Syrian armies to the June 10, 1967 cease-fire lines. The stance represented a final provocation to the Arabs and evoked their OPEC decision of October 17, imposing a boycott of oil on the Netherlands.

This sanction quickly brought the Dutch government in line with the rest of Europe. Thus, it was prepared to accept France's initiative in adopting a pro-Palestinian stance.

Western Europe imported sixty-five percent of its oil from the Middle East and North Africa. As fighting began, the oil ministers of the Arab OPEC nations gathered in Kuwait on October 17 and swiftly agreed to reduce their oil consignments to the West. The ministers then established categories for the various purchasing nations, linking their oil quotas to their support of the Arab cause. Under these OPEC guidelines, then, France was virtually exempted from the ban. Conversely, a total embargo was imposed on both the United States and the Netherlands.

But when a second Arab meeting took place in Kuwait on December 9, 1973, and the Arab ministers decided to apply the next reduction in deliveries to all countries, friendly, neutral, or hostile alike, it became clear that the war simply had offered the Gulf oil nations their pretext for cutting production and raising prices.

In Brussels, to placate the Arabs, the European representatives agreed to endorse a Franco-British text that went much further than the Schumann report of 1971. Urging "a just and lasting peace" based on UN Security Council Resolution 242, their declaration now also recommended that a settlement ensure the "legitimate rights of the Palestinians," and an Israeli withdrawal from occupied lands. In a further genuflection to the Arabs, the statement offered two additional proposals: that the Arab-Israeli negotiations take place within the framework of the UN; and that a peace settlement include "international guarantees," a concept that implied either UN or

Soviet participation. The second meeting of the EU foreign ministers in Copenhagen on December 14 essentially reinforced the Brussels declaration. Yet, in still another departure from earlier norms, the EC this time invited the Arab ministers to attend the conference as "observers," for the purpose of developing "closer understanding and cooperation" between the Europeans and the Arab world.

Neither the Brussels nor the Copenhagen declaration eased the OPEC oil escalations.

Henry Kissinger's efforts to coordinate Western oil policy fell flat. The EC followed the French lead, accepted the Arab agenda, and exerted pressure on Israel to accommodate the "legitimate needs of the Palestinians."

During the autumn of 1979 the EC agreed to develop a relationship with the PLO. To that end, in November 1979 Giscard invited Yasser Arafat for an official visit to Paris. The news infuriated Meir Rosenne, Israel's ambassador to Paris. During a television interview he all but exploded: "I refuse to believe that the land of the Declaration of the Rights of Man would invite a terrorist. Would France invite Hitler?"

Meanwhile, as the peace process underwent its tortuous ordeal in bilateral Egyptian-Israeli meetings from the end of 1977 to early 1979, the Europeans were stunned in March 1979 when the Egyptian president consented to a peace treaty with Israel. Sadat himself requested that the EU exercise restraint, to allow Washington to broker the peace. Afterwards, as it became increasingly clear that Egyptian-Israeli negotiations on Palestine were at an impasse, France once again defended "the legitimacy of a Palestinian homeland," while Italy, Britain and the Netherlands spoke of the Palestinian people's right to a "national identity" and offered to help fund a self-governing enterprise. Their expressions were intensified by the Arab world's execration of Sadat for his "sellout."

After joining the EC, Denmark accepted the EC line, including the 1980 Venice Declaration. As for Sweden, no government in Europe was harsher in its criticism of the Jewish State than that of Swedish Prime Minister Olaf Palme. During Palme's tenure, between 1982 and 1986, Swedish antipathy to Israeli "oppression" had become so vocal and so indiscriminate that Israel's ambassador to Stockholm persuaded Jerusalem simply to abandon its political dialogue with the Palme government.

"Occupied Territories" A Repeated Lie. Evelyn Gordon in the *Jerusalem Post*, August 13, 2002:

> "US Secretary of Defense Donald Rumsfeld shocked the world last week when he referred to Israel's 'so-called occupation' of the West Bank and Gaza. By implying that he does not consider Israel's presence in these territories to be an illegal occupation, Rumsfeld denied one of the modern world's most widely accepted dogmas. Yet the very fact that his statement was received as little short of heretical begs an obvious question: How did a label with not a shred of basis in international law turn into such a universal truth?

> "The standard definition of occupation under international law is found in the Fourth Geneva Convention, which applies explicitly to 'partial or total occupation of the territory of a high contracting party.'

In other words the 'occupation' for the purpose of the convention means the presence of one country's troops in territory that belongs to another sovereign state – the only type of entity that can be a contracting party to the convention.

"But when territory that does not clearly belong to another sovereign state is captured by one of the possible legitimate claimants, as for instance in Kashmir, which is claimed by India, Pakistan and the Kashmirs, the term generally used is 'disputed,' not 'occupied.' And that is precisely the situation in West Bank and Gaza. Neither of these territories belonged to any sovereign state when Israel captured them in 1967; they were essentially stateless territory. Both had originally been part of the League of Nations Mandate for Palestine and, according to the UN partition plan of 1947, they should have become part of a new Arab state when Britain abandoned the Mandate in 1948.

"But since the Arabs themselves rejected this plan, not only did that state never come into being, it never even acquired theoretical legitimacy: The partition plan was no more than a non-binding 'recommendation' (the resolution's own language) adopted by the General Assembly. Once rejected by one of the parties involved, it essentially became a dead letter.

"The West Bank and Gaza were therefore not owned by anyone when they were seized by Jordan and Egypt, respectively, in 1948; and since their annexation by these countries was never internationally recognized (Jordan's annexation of the West Bank was accepted only by Britain and Pakistan) they were stateless territory in 1967. Moreover, Israel had a very strong claim to both territories. Even aside from the obvious historical claim (the heart of the biblical kingdom of Israel was in what is now called the West Bank), the terms of the original League of Nations Mandate quite clearly assigned the West Bank and Gaza to the Jewish state.

"The preamble to the Mandate explicitly stated that its purpose was the 'establishment in Palestine of a national home for the Jewish people.' How, then, did the myth of 'occupation' – i.e., that these territories indisputably belong to someone other than Israel – gain such universal credence? Sadly, the main culprit is Israel itself. Since no third party could be expected to press a claim that Israel refused to press for itself, the Arab claim, by default, became the only one on the international agenda."

Operation Peace for the Galilee

In reaction to the incessant Katyusha rocket bombings of Israeli border towns, Prime Minster Menahem Begin ordered a full-scale military invasion of Southern Lebanon, with the intent of destroying the PLO's extensive infrastructure of terrorist bases and ultimately eradicating the PLO as a political force. In ensuing weeks, however, with PLO terrorists retreating to safe positions in the Moslem sector of West Beirut, the Israeli invasion evolved into a congested siege, replete with air bombardments that devastated civilian and military enclaves alike, inflicting many hundreds of casualties. Not until August 12, 1982 did a cease-fire come into effect. Brokered by the US, it permitted Arafat and his terrorists and his headquarters to leave Beirut, transferring them to other Arab lands.

Civil war between Moslems and Christians was an old story in Lebanon. During the 1970s, fighting between the two communities had devoured thousands of lives. Nevertheless, for the Europeans, the intramural carnage had evoked little more than a fatigued sense of apathy. But this time, when it involved Jews, the reaction was quite different. Western newspapers and television reportage gave sharply biased accounts of the war. Journalists drew portentous analogies between the "genocide" of Beirut and the genocide of Warsaw in World War II. On June 9, the European community denounced the invasion as a "flagrant violation of international law and of the most basic humanitarian principles."

In West Germany, the upsurge of anti-Israeli and even anti-Semitic sentiment became quite palpable. In February 1983, a leading German poll hinted at a sharp decline in Israeli-German relations, as fifty-two percent of respondents agreed that "we should not place our good relations with Israel above all else. The Arab countries are important for our oil needs. Therefore, we should not become enemies of these countries on Israel's account." Only eighteen percent favored the alternative choice: "It is still important today for the Federal Republic of Germany to attend to its specially friendly relations with Israel."

At a Council of Ministers gathering in Brussels on June 17, Greek Prime Minister Papandreou characterized Israel's invasion as "Nazi" and "Fascist." It was Germany's Chancellor Schmidt who protested that such terms should be banned from EC discussions. The British ambassador to the Security Council, too, harshly criticized Israel, for "taking the law in its own hands in someone else's territory." It was then, too, that London reimposed its 1973 arms embargo against Israel.

On June 15, 1982, French President Mitterrand firmly rebuffed Israel's foreign minister, Yitzhak Shamir, who had flown to Paris in quest of the president's understanding. Nine days later, entreating the EC to request an immediate withdrawal of Israeli troops from Lebanon, Mitterrand went so far as to compare Israel's "smash-up" offensive through Lebanon with the Nazi wartime destruction of the French village of Ouradour.

CHAPTER FIVE

Europe and the Arab Boycott

Economic isolation in the long run proved by far more painful than political ostracization. From 1949 on, Egypt blocked the Suez Canal not only to Israeli ships but to selected cargoes carried by vessels of other nations bound for the Jewish state. The closure of the Suez in and of itself was less than crippling to the Israeli economy. Rather, it was a wider economic boycott that exerted a more invidious, longer-lived impact. The quarantine was launched in 1951, when the Arab League organized a Central Boycott Office in Damascus with branch offices in other member states. Initially the proscription on economic dealings with Israel was intended for the Arab countries themselves. Little time passed, however, before the boycott was extended to other nations.

The ban was imposed first and foremost on non-Israeli vessels that stopped at Israeli ports. The Boycott Office maintained a detailed blacklist of these transgressors, and over the next three decades more than six hundred ships fell under the ban. Henceforth, they were denied access to any Arab port.

Shipping companies soon learned to adapt to these regulations by allocating certain vessels, often under charter of fake registrations, exclusively to the Israeli run. But in 1953, the Boycott Office extended its restrictions to foreign airlines stopping in Israel. No plane flying to or from Israel was allowed to continue over Arab airspace to any other destination, Arab or non-Arab. Most Western airlines were obliged to terminate their eastern schedules at Israel's Lod Airport, then return directly to their home bases. Ticket prices reflected this economic function. In practice, every overseas Arab embassy and consulate operated as a branch of the Boycott Office. These branches in turn played a crucial role in developing a new secondary boycott on Israel. The technique was to gather data on foreign companies, even to circulate questionnaires among them, to determine which were doing business with Israel; which maintained factories, plants, or agencies in Israel; and which sold Israeli patents, copyrights or trademarks, or purchased shares in Israel enterprises. Once included in the office's black list, a foreign company was promptly denied access to the Arab market. It was a price few businesses were willing to pay. To circumvent the boycott, Israeli companies were obliged to make their purchases or sales through dummy agencies. The price in extra commissions was high. This secondary boycott proved by far the most effective. No nation, no company, however large or powerful, was exempt from its operation.

On signing the 1953 Treaty of Luxembourg, West Germany became a logical early target. Yet Chancellor Konrad Adenauer declared that "it would be shameful indeed, if we were to waver in our decision only because we are threatened with economic disadvantages. There are higher values than good business deals." But the chancellor was speaking for his government, and not for private German businesses. Under German law they were entitled to make their own decisions. While a number of German corporations defied the ban, no fewer than two hundred companies complied over the ensuing three decades, and these included such heavyweights as Telefunken, BASF, and Siemens.

From its outset in 1951, the boycott operated with even greater effect in Britain, the nation with which Israel had developed its most extensive trade connections since the earliest years of the Palestine mandate. Like Bonn, Britain refused officially to participate in the quarantine. Yet it could hardly bar individual companies from pursuing their own opportunities in the Middle East. From 1951, a substantial majority of Britain's larger companies sooner or later capitulated to the boycott, and these included such giants as Shell, British Petroleum, and the largest number of banks and insurance firms. The ban also extended to companies owned, or partly owned, by Jews. In a particularly notorious episode, the Boycott Office in 1963 coerced the Norwich Union Insurance Society into dropping Lord Mancroft, a Jew and former minister in the Macmillan government, from its board of directors.

In France, too, even in the apogee of the French-Israeli honeymoon, hundreds of companies surrendered to boycott pressures. In 1957, the Renault automobile company agreed to sublicense assembly rights to an Israeli company. Two years later, threatened by the Boycott Office, Renault summarily canceled the contract. Renault was a nationalized firm, and the cancellation plainly had been decided on the governmental level. Long-term credits no longer were extended for Israeli purchases of French equipment. The interdiction against firms with Jewish ownership, or part ownership, also was applied in France. Finally, in June 1977, under heavy pressure from the Carter administration, the French National Assembly passed a mild form of anti-boycott legislation. It forbade compliance with inquiries relating to "national origin, or membership or non-membership in a particular ethnic group, race, or religion." But a year later Prime Minister Raymond Barre issued a decree that seriously undermined this legislation; and in May 1980 the Giscard d'Estaing government specified that any commercial transaction relating to energy, agriculture, minerals, transportation, machine and consumer goods – in effect everything – was to be excluded from the 1977 law.

Meanwhile, the Netherlands, Denmark, Belgium and Norway were helpless to block private businesses from exercising their own discretion in buying or selling in the Middle East. The boycott's ramifications penetrated every corner of the European economy. The damage to the Israeli economy was heavy. An Israeli finance ministry report covering the period 1972-83 estimated that as the consequence of Arab economic warfare, the nation in these years had lost more than six billion dollars in exports.

Without exception, Europe's statesmen favored the promotion of trade links as a means of fostering political stability in the Mediterranean. As early as 1961, the EEC Council of Ministers authorized the Commission's technocrats to study a possible relationship with the Mediterranean "poor cousins." And Israel too, then, became an object of EC evaluation. Campaigning behind the scene on Israel's behalf, Belgium's

Foreign Minister Spak won the unanimous support of the Benelux trading consortium.

Even with this approbation, however, and that of West Germany, the maximum the Community appeared willing to offer was a tightly limited commercial agreement. The deal was a modest one. It reduced the ECC's duties on such traditional Israeli products as grapefruit, avocados, and plywood. The document also confirmed that Israel would share in whichever duty reductions might be later extended to other Mediterranean nations, including Italy and Spain. For the Jewish State it was a meaningful foot in the European door.

In 1975, the European Community awarded Israel a form of de facto associate status. Israel appeared to have profited handsomely from that connection. Its trade deficit with Europe was reduced. Its industry grew and diversified. Yet the progress was uneven. Israeli agriculture was encountering formidable competition from the subtropical produce of Italy and Greece. Upon becoming members of the EC, Spain and Portugal would be eligible for EC subsidies that were certain to erode Israel's competitiveness even further.

A major additional protocol to the treaty was signed by the European Commission in December 1987. In essence, the amendment permitted Israeli agricultural exports a grace period before the EC's subsidies of Spanish and Portuguese imports came into effect. At the same time, the European Commission lowered its tariffs and enlarged both the quotas and categories of Israeli agricultural imports.

However, in March 1988 the European parliament announced that it was withholding ratification of the Israeli protocol. The veto was intended as a political statement of support for the Palestinians. Israeli friends in Germany then dutifully interceded with their colleagues. Thus, in October 1988 the European parliament ended its "sanction" by assenting to the protocol. Yet in February 1990, complying with still another parliamentary recommendation, the EC imposed a new series of restrictive measures. These blocked Israel's access to some fifteen projects submitted by the EC-Israel Joint Scientific Committee, and postponed a cooperative agreement in the field of energy. Within a year most of them were reversed.

CHAPTER SIX

Arab Terror in Europe

In the West Bank, Israeli security forces easily suppressed isolated outbursts of Palestinian violence. It was rather beyond its own frontiers that the Jewish State and the Jewish people proved vulnerable.

On July 22, 1968, an El Al flight en route from Rome to Tel Aviv was hijacked by two Arab passengers, members of the Popular Front for the Liberation of Palestine, a leftist PLO faction. The terrorists forced the crew to fly the plane to Algiers. There, twelve Israeli passengers were held hostage in exchange for the release of fifteen Palestinians incarcerated in Israeli prisons, and a five million dollar ransom. After thirty-nine days, Israel agreed to the exchange and the payment.

The July 1968, hijacking in fact soon triggered a chain reaction of terrorist assaults on El Al, then on other airlines with service to Israel, and ultimately on Israeli civilians in Europe. At Athens airport on December 26, 1968, a trio of PFLP terrorists let loose a spray of automatic-weapon fire at a crowd of passengers awaiting an El Al flight. Two Israelis were hit, one fatally. At this point, aware that PFLP training bases were concentrated in Lebanon, the Israeli government two days later launched its devastating commando raid on Beirut airport, blowing up thirteen passenger jets of Lebanon's national airline. Western reaction was not forbearing. The UN Security Council vigorously condemned Israel. De Gaulle found his pretext for canceling the Mirage fighter contract.

In February 1969, Palestinians fired at an El Al plane loading passengers at Zurich airport. A crewmember was killed. In August 1969, a TWA plane en route from Paris to Tel Aviv was hijacked and diverted to Damascus, where four Israeli male passengers were imprisoned. In November of the same year, an Arab terrorist threw grenades at the El Al office in Athens, wounding fourteen people and killing a Greek infant. Shortly afterward, three Arabs fired at passengers waiting to board an El Al flight at Munich airport. An Israeli was killed, and Israeli actress, Hannah Meron, lost a leg. In February 1970, terrorists planted a bomb on a Swissair plane destined for Tel Aviv. The jet blew up midair, and sixteen Israelis were among its forty-seven victims.

On September 2, 1970, Palestinians hijacked an El Al plane en route from Amsterdam to New York. The airline crew managed to subdue the two attackers, killing the man and wounding his companion. The plane made an emergency descent in London. As it rolled to a stop at Heathrow airport, an urgent message arrived from Israel, ordering the El Al captain to take off immediately for Tel Aviv: Israeli intelligence wished to interrogate the surviving hijacker, Leila Khaled. The British police intervened, refusing to allow the plane to depart until they took the young woman into their own custody. Four days later, teams of Palestinian terrorists hijacked three passenger jets, belonging to BOAC, TWA, and Swissair, and forced their crews to land at an abandoned desert airstrip near Zerqa, Jordan. There, three hundred and ten passengers became hostages to be exchanged for some two hundred Palestinian prisoners in Israel, as well as for Leila Khaled in Britain, and for a dozen other Arab terrorists in Switzerland and Germany. Unless the prisoners were released within seventy-two hours, warned the hijackers, all the planes would be blown up, together with their passengers and crews.

The British, Swiss and German governments were prepared to comply. Not so Israel. After seventy-two hours of silence from Jerusalem, the Palestinians at Zerqa began to waver. Jordan's King Hussein also had warned that he was prepared to use force against them, and his troops appeared to be closing a ring around the captive airliners. The terrorists then evacuated the passengers, blew up the planes, and carried off the hostages to isolated holding pens. Still Israel held firm. In the end the hijackers wilted, accepting as their quid pro quo the release exclusively of Arab prisoners in European prisons.

In May 1972, an elite PLO shock contingent, "Black September," managed to hijack a Sabena airliner shortly after its take off from Brussels en route to Tel Aviv. The four terrorists – two men and two women – ordered the crew to continue its scheduled flight to Israel. Upon landing at Lod Airport, the hijackers threatened to blow up the plane with its ninety-three passengers unless prisoners in Israeli prisons were released and brought directly to the plane, which would then fly on to Cairo. The Israeli reaction was characteristic. Within hours their commandos stormed and recaptured the aircraft. Although one passenger was killed, both male Palestinians were shot dead and the two women terrorists were taken prisoner. Under interrogation it became clear then that Europe had been targeted as the principal battleground for operations against Israel.

In the ensuing months of 1972-73, an unfolding series of terrorists attacks confirmed these intelligence findings. A letter bomb killed the Israeli agricultural attaché in London. Bombs exploded at the Israeli embassy in Brussels, grenades were thrown at an El Al office injuring four Belgians. Worse yet, no European government seemed willing to impose heavy punishment on convicted Arab killers. Rather, it was revealed later that Lufthansa had entered into detailed negotiations with several Arab organizations to ensure the safety of its flights; even as France's Pompidou government negotiated a "gentleman's agreement" with the PLO to refrain from assaults on Air France flights.

By early 1970, several factors evidently had transformed Western Europe into an ideal staging grounds for Israel's enemies: large communities of Palestinians and other Arabs lived in these countries as students, workers or transient businessmen; Western Europe offered geographic proximity and excellent transportation facilities that permitted rapid cross-border movement; it offered, too, an abundance of targets, as in the network of diplomatic and commercial offices of local Jewish business and communal institutions. The security of Israelis or of other Jews was not the central preoccupation of Western European governments. No one could comprehend Europe's pusillanimity in coping with the violence in its midst.

The rise of the Black September movement had far-reaching consequences for escalating Middle East terrorism. Created by Yasser Arafat and Ali Hassan Salameh, an ardent volunteer in

Fatah and son of the infamous Hassan Salameh (one of the most effective and cruel commandos during the Palestine War of 1947-48), Black September – named for a September massacre of Palestinians in Jordan – served as an instrument of revenge against "the enemies of the Palestinian people." As chief of Black September operations, Salameh promptly embarked on his mission with a ferocity and dynamism that transcended even his late father's. He negotiated a partnership with other guerilla cabals, such as George Habash's Popular Front for the Liberation of Palestine, and with non-Arab terrorists outfits like Germany's Baader-Meinhof gang, the Japanese Red Army, Iran's Liberation Front and Turkey's People's Liberation army. Each shared with the others its intelligence information, its training techniques, its safe houses in various European cities.

On May 30, 1972, Air France flight 132 arrived in Israel after a stopover in Rome; three disembarking passengers, members of the Japanese Red Army, opened their hand luggage, pulled out submachine guns, and coolly slaughtered twenty-six people and wounded seventy-two others in the terminal before Israeli police wounded and captured them. Ironically, most of the victims were Puerto Ricans arriving as pilgrims to visit the Christian shrines in the Holy Land.

The Munich Slaughter

On August 23, 1972, a Palestinian couple landed in Cologne, Germany. Their hand baggage went unsearched. The couple then rented an automobile and drove to Munich. As the site of the Olympics, scheduled to begin on September 1, the Bavarian capital was a logical tourist magnet that summer. Once in Munich the couple transferred their luggage to the local Black

September commander, Muhammad Massalha. With him were seven other Palestinians who had trained with him in Lebanon. Their objective was nothing less than the capture of Israel's entire Olympic team. Ali Hassan Salameh flew to communist East Germany, taking up his "command post" in a rented East Berlin apartment.

On September 5, donning ski masks, Massalha and his fellow seven guerrillas climbed the fence into the Olympic Village, made their way to the targeted building and swiftly ascended to the complex of the third floor lodgings where the Israeli athletes were housed. There, the Palestinians succeeded in blasting open one of the apartment doors with gunfire. The Israeli wrestling team was inside. Some of the athletes managed to jump through windows and escape, but two were killed and nine captured. Massalha then appeared at an open window and threw out a typed declaration containing his group's demands. Within minutes the building was surrounded by a massive police cordon. Chancellor Willy Brandt ordered the negotiation of a peaceful solution. At the same time Brandt telephoned Prime Minister Golda Meir in Jerusalem, inviting the cooperation of the Israeli government. The chancellor was hardly surprised that Mrs. Meir rejected any notion of capitulating to the terrorists' demands. Stalling for time, the German authorities engaged in tedious negotiations with the terrorists. Ali Hassan Salameh authorized Massalha to extend his deadline several times. All the while, over Israel's objections, Brandt allowed the Olympic games to continue.

Massalha approved an agreement whereby Israel would liberate some fifty Palestinians from its prisons. In fact neither Brandt nor Golda Meir intended to honor the agreement. The terrorists would be seized before they left German soil. But Israel had expected the police to launch their assault on the Palestinians the moment they departed their apartment building. Instead, the German scenario was to rescue the hostages only after they had been carried by two helicopters from the Olympic Village to the neighboring airforce base. Once the Arabs descended from the helicopters and continued by foot to the bus assigned to drive them to an awaiting Lufthansa jet, they would be picked off by police snipers.

Matters did not work out as planned. Upon landing Massalha smelled a rat: The distance to the waiting bus was suspiciously long. He ordered the other seven terrorists to remain in the helicopters with the hostages. For the police sharpshooters, waiting on the roof of the terminal, it was then or never. The police opened fire, killing Massalha and wounding one of his companions. Thereupon the other Palestinians fired long bursts at their Israeli hostages, killing them all. As a result, the clumsy ambush had left all nine Israelis dead, together with Massalha, five of the seven terrorists and one German policeman.

The bitterness left in Israeli mouths became gall only three weeks later. Bonn exchanged the two Palestinians who had been captured alive for a Lufthansa plane that had been "hijacked" over the Mediterranean, flying them off to Libya whence they were transported to Damascus and a hero's welcome. In its fury at this palpable German-Arab collusion, Israel briefly recalled its ambassador to Bonn for "consultations."

The Mossad established a secret committee with the mandate of identifying, targeting, and eliminating those responsible for the string of murders against Israeli civilians overseas, and specifically for the Munich Olympic massacre. Less than two weeks passed before the first operation was approved. The intended target was Walid Zwaiter. Posting as a translator for the Libyan embassy in Rome, Zwaiter was in fact a Palestinian who directed Black September's key operational base in Europe. Rome suited the terrorists' purposes almost ideally. Its airport was nearly as inefficient as Athens' in its haphazard security precautions. Terrorists easily smuggled weapons in and out of the airport's terminals. On October 16, returning home in mid-evening, Zwaiter was shot dead at the entrance to his apartment.

Upon returning home in the early evening, Mahmud Hamshari, a second-ranking Black September operative in Europe, picked up the receiver of his telephone and was killed by a concealed bomb. Hussein Abd al Quir, a senior figure in the Black September organization, was killed by a booby-trapped bed in a hotel room.

In March 1973, Ali Hassan Salameh devised a plan to hijack a commercial aircraft in Europe, fly it to Tripoli, Libya, load it with explosives, and then have it flown to Tel Aviv by a suicide commando. Coordinator of the operation would be Dr. Basil al-Qubaissi, a professor at the American University in Beirut who recently had arrived in Paris to fill the vacuum left by the assassinated Hamshari. On April 6, two Israeli agents sauntered by Qubaissi's apartment building as he was returning from his office and calmly shot him to death.

In Cyprus, the very next day, a new Black September agent, who had been sent to replace the assassinated Abd al Quir, returned to his Nicosia hotel room, turned on the light, and died in an explosion – exactly as his predecessor had.

These successes did not lessen the Mossad's endless frustration by their inability to track down Ali Hassan Salameh himself. In January 1973, Salameh planned an audacious operation to kill Prime Minister Golda Meir upon her arrival in Rome for an audience with Pope Paul VI. Mrs. Meir's aircraft would be shot down as it descended at the Rome airport. Pursuing every lead, the Mossad was still unable to locate the weapons; no missiles were found. On the day of Mrs. Meir's scheduled arrival the situation was unbearably tense. Indeed, the Prime Minister's El Al jet was actually on its final descent when one of the agents, scouting a perimeter highway in his automobile, suddenly noticed an anomaly in a food concession cart by the side of the road. There were three stacks poking out of its roof, but only one was smoking. The Israeli did a sharp U-turn on the road and crashed his automobile directly into the cart, turning it over and pinning two of its five occupants beneath it. Climbing out, the Israeli confirmed that the men were all Arabs, and that there were missiles inside. The surviving plotters were arrested.

In January 1973, a senior Mossad agent in Madrid, Baruch Cohen, was lured to a meeting at a café by one of his Arab informers. There he was ambushed by Black September gunmen and shot dead. In March Palestinian gunmen killed an Israeli businessman in Cyprus; in April an Italian employee of El Al was killed in Rome. On April 9, the Palestinians came within minutes of wiping out the Israeli ambassador and his family in Nicosia. At the Vienna airport, a week later, also at the last minute, sky marshals intercepted a trio of Arabs as they prepared to blow up an El Al jet.

By spring 1973, Salameh's principal operatives in Rome, Paris, Athens, Nicosia and Beirut had been liquidated.

However, there was no lack of other Palestinian groups; on July 1, a Palestinian waylaid Israel's attaché in Washington, shooting him dead outside his suburban home. In August two Palestinians attacked a TWA plane in Athens just as it landed on a flight from Tel Aviv, killing five passengers and wounding four.

On September 28, 1973, three armed Arabs slipped aboard a Soviet train carrying Jewish emigrés to Vienna. As the train entered Austrian territory, the Arabs seized five Jews and a customs official as hostages, then demanded air passage to an Arab capital. In fact they got more than they asked for: Austrian Chancellor Bruno Kreisky ordered closure of the transit center in which the Jewish Agency housed and classified Soviet Jews before flying them off to Israel. Soon afterward the terrorists released the hostages, who were themselves then flown out of Vienna to Libya.

Nine days later the Yom Kippur war erupted. A certain lull followed the Yom Kippur War, yet there were occasional assaults on Israelis abroad. At the Istanbul air terminal in August 1976, two PFLP members opened fire at passengers waiting to board an El Al flight to Tel Aviv, killing four people and wounding twenty-six. In January, Palestinian terrorists blew up part of the Mount Royal Hotel in London, the residence of several Israeli diplomatic staffers.

In March, an Arab terrorist assassinated a Spanish lawyer in Madrid, whom he misidentified as a Jewish leader.

In April, inspecting baggage intended for an El Al airliner in Zurich, security agents detected and disarmed a suitcase bomb wired to an altimeter. In July, acting on a tip, police in Copenhagen arrested a group of terrorists preparing an attack on an El Al crew. Also in July, a Palestinian was arrested before he could hurl his grenades at El Al passengers in Brussels airport. On July 27, a grenade attack on a Jewish school in Antwerp left one child dead and thirteen wounded.

In Paris, a bomb exploded outside a synagogue on Rue Copernic, killing four people and injuring thirteen.

In London, on June 3, 1982, a Palestinian shot and gravely wounded the Israeli ambassador, Shlomo Argov. The assailant was caught, and within hours police tracked down and arrested three of his Arab colleagues, together with substantial quantities of weapons. In September, Arab terrorists threw a hand grenade at the El Al office in Paris, killing two passersby and wounding twelve. In December, a group of Palestinians machined-gunned the corridor near the El Al ticketing area at Rome's airport, killing thirty-two passengers and injuring forty. By then, except for Ali Hassan Salameh himself, the Black September command had been all but shattered. In 1978, at long last, the Mossad found its chance.

That year Salameh married a Lebanese beauty, a former Miss Universe. Living in Beirut, Salameh traveled between his home and his wife's apartment near Black September headquarters on Rue Verdun. His schedule, increasingly predictable, was duly noted. In January 1979 a Mossad agent planted a small tracking radio transmitter under Salameh's automobile. Two weeks later, Salameh's car exploded; Salameh, his bodyguards, and several passersby were blown to bits.

Italy

The nation's wartime record on behalf of European Jewry was humane, even noble, and hardly less so in facilitating the transport of refugee Jews to Israel. Italy's cabinets of the next decades, loosely associated with the Vatican and with the nation's larger business interests, were not unfriendly toward Israel. In 1947-48, as a defeated Axis power, Italy was excluded from the United Nations voting on partition; but in 1949 it extended de facto recognition to Israel and de jure recognition a year later. From 1951 on, Italian ambassadors presented their credentials to the president of Israel in Jerusalem (over the reservations of the Vatican).

During the 1980s Libya provided up to half of Italy's oil imports. Three-quarters of Italy's gas imports came from Algeria. In reaction then to the Arab oil embargo during the 1973 Yom Kippur War, Italy's relations with Israel suddenly deteriorated. In ensuing years, whether as prime minister or foreign minister, Giulio Andreotti was a perennial in his nation's Christian Democratic cabinets. It was thus at Andreotti's initiative that the government enhanced its relationship with the PLO, authorized the opening of a PLO office in Rome, and finally invited Yasser Arafat to an official reception at the president's palace. It was a stance that contrasted sharply with the cooperation that in earlier years had existed between the Italian secret service and the Mossad. Under heavy economic and diplomatic pressure from Libya's Qaddafi, the Italian government released the prisoners of the aborted missile attack on Golda Meir's plane in November of the same year, then arranged for them to be flown secretly to Benghazi. Other Palestinians seized following acts of terrorism against Israelis or other Jews on Italian soil, were dutifully arrested, tried, and incarcerated. But most served only partial sentences before being repatriated to Arab countries.

On October 7, 1985, a group of Arab terrorists commandeered the Italian cruise ship *Achille Lauro*, en route from Alexandria to Port Said. Five hundred passengers were on board, most American. The terrorists radioed an ultimatum that the civilians would be detained until fifty prisoners in Israel were released. Rome ordered Italian naval units to converge on the ship.

Early on the morning of October 9, the Palestinians radioed a second ultimatum. If their demands were not met by midnight, they warned, they would begin executing hostages. Agreement, then, was reached to allow the notorious PLF chieftain Abu Abbas to serve as mediator, and he was promptly flown into Cairo from Baghdad. Soon afterward, in the course of frenzied negotiations among Cairo, Rome, Washington, and the *Achille Lauro* hijackers, a deal was reached. Provided the ship was released, with all its passengers unharmed, the four Palestinians would be turned over to Egypt. President Mubarak, in turn, would guarantee them safe passage to an Arab country of their choice.

On the same afternoon of October 9, the hijackers gave up control of the *Achille Lauro* and Andreotti confirmed to Washington that the passengers were all safe. Immediately, the four Arabs were turned over to the Egyptian authorities, which prepared to fly them out of the country, together with Abu Abas. It is virtually certain that Mubarak, and probably even Andreotti, already possessed information they did not share with the United States: Only hours before the vessel was released, the hijackers had shot an aged and infirm American Jewish passenger, Leon Klinghoffer, and dumped his body into the sea. On boarding the ship at 11:00 p.m., American ambassador Nicholas Veliotis belatedly learned of the tragedy. Furious, he demanded that Cairo turn the hijackers over to American custody forthwith.

Secretly, in the early evening of October 10, an Egyptian Boeing 737 carrying the four hijackers and Abu Abas departed from Cairo for Tunis. When the Tunisian government refused it permission to land, the plane made for Algiers. Once again landing permission was denied. The Boeing then headed back to Cairo. During the entire odyssey, President Mubarak blandly assured American Ambassador Veliotis that the hijackers remained in Egyptian custody. But an Israeli intelligence officer had intercepted the airliner's radio transmission and alerted the CIA. The Reagan Administration promptly instructed carrier jets of the United States Sixth Fleet to intercept the Egyptian airliner, ordering the Egyptian crew to follow their escort to the American NATO base in Italy.

During these same hours, Prime Minister Craxi and Foreign Minister Andreotti preened in self-congratulation that their diplomacy had won a "great victory," proving that Italy exerted influence with the Arabs, even with their terrorist organizations. Indeed, only the week before, Craxi had condemned, as a "terrorist action," Israel's bombing of PLO headquarters outside Tunis. Andreotti equated the raid with the wartime Nazi massacre of Jews hiding in the catacombs of Rome. But now, shortly after midnight on October 11, US Secretary of State George Shultz reached Andreotti by phone to alert him that the hijackers were en route to the NATO base, and that Washington insisted they be brought to the United States for trial under the American-Italian extradition treaty.

A grave crisis ensued between the two countries. Italian troops were alerted to surround the Egyptian Boeing as it landed at the base. Yet the American escort planes disgorged several hundred American commandos, who promptly surrounded the fifty-man Italian contingent. Hours of tense Washington-Rome negotiations followed. In mid-afternoon, President Reagan telephoned Mr. Craxi personally to request the extradition of the terrorists. After another day of back-and-forth discussions, a compromise again was reached. Rome gave its solemn assurance that it would prosecute the terrorists to the full extent of the law, provided they were allowed to remain in Italian custody. Washington was less concerned with the four hijackers than with Abu Abas, who had accompanied the terrorists on the Egyptian airliner. The United States wanted assurances that Abu Abas would be held in custody and aggressively prosecuted. At this point, however, President Mubarak insisted that Abu Abas was under Egyptian diplomatic protection. Mubarak warned that he would not release the ship, still in Egyptian waters, to Italy until Abu Abas was released. Repeatedly the Italians protested to Washington that their commitment to incarceration and prosecution had not applied to Abu Abas. Upon confirming this Italian position, Mubarak then released the ship. Meanwhile, the five Arabs had already been flown in an Italian aircraft from the base to Rome, where they were jailed. Prime Minister Craxi then had Abu Abas rushed to Fiumicino airport, escorted to a Yugoslav airliner, and flown out of the country. Denouncing the premier's "abject capitulation to international terrorism," Defense Minister

Spadolini on October 14 pulled his Republican colleagues out of the Craxi cabinet, and the Italian government collapsed.

Eventually it was restructured. Among its foreign policy commitments, the program emphasized non-capitulation to blackmail by international terrorists, and stern condemnation of the violence used by the Palestinian organizations.

Spain

Spain functioned as a haven for terrorists of all backgrounds. In October 1984, two Israeli sailors were murdered in Barcelona. The Costa del Sol became a favored site for assassination attempts against Israelis and vacationing European Jews.

Turkey

In September 1986, Arab terrorists slaughtered twenty-two worshippers in Istanbul's Neve Shalom Synagogue.

Greece

The longstanding conflict between Judaism and Byzantium provided an appropriate backdrop for Greek anti-Semitism in the post World War I years, and Greek diplomatic hostility in the post World War II years. From the moment the Palestine issue reached the United Nations in 1947, Athens vigorously opposed partition; and during the ensuing 1948-49 war, its support of the Arab cause was flagrant and even collaborative. The Greek government banned passage through its territory to volunteers or material destined for Israel, although not for concomitant support to the Arab nations. For several years even after Israel's birth, Israeli citizens on foreign airlines were not so much as allowed to leave their planes during stopovers at Athens Airport.

Yet it was counterproductive for Greece to withhold diplomatic recognition of Israel altogether. The Orthodox Church network of institutions in Jerusalem required the presence of a Greek consul general in the Holy City. Israel, in turn, eager to foster those official contacts, was prepared to guarantee Greek Orthodox access to Christian shrines against encroachments by the Latins; while, for its part, the Orthodox Patriarchate entered an expedient alliance with Israel in opposing a Corpus Separatum for Jerusalem. Except for the Jerusalem relationship, however, formal contacts between the two governments remained minimal. Refusing to countenance an ambassadorial exchange with the Jewish State, the Greeks permitted Israel no more than a legation in Athens, and, at that accredited the Israeli emissary simply as a "diplomatic representative." In its coverage of the Arab-Israeli impasse, the Greek press hewed unremittingly to the Arab line.

Greek shippers relied on Arab oil traffic, an income source they did not dare jeopardize. Most decisively, the Cyprus issue determined Greece's Middle Eastern policy. For Athens, assurance of support from the powerful Arab bloc in the United Nations demanded a reciprocal endorsement of Arab claims against Israel.

Even Nasser's harshly xenophobic laws of 1956-57, a series of property confiscation and punitive taxes that soon reduced Egypt's Greek population to less than thirty thousand from one hundred and fourty thousand, would not shake Athens' stance on Israel. Whether on the issues of Israeli-Arab border violence, Palestinian refugees, or the status of Jerusalem, Greek support for the Arabs was reflexive. By the mid-1950s, Israel had come to regard Greece as a de facto member of the Arab League, and hardly worth consulting any longer, let alone cultivating. Diplomatic contacts between the two nations remained perfunctory, year after year. Trade between them was negligible.

In 1981, the New Democrats lost a national election to PASOK, the Socialist party. Under the leadership of Andreas Papandreou, a fiery doctrinaire leftist, Athens adopted a resentful attitude toward NATO and the European community, both of which it regarded as under "imperialist" American influence. Israel, regarded as a "puppet" of American imperialism, was vulnerable to Papandreou's inflammatory rhetoric. Its post-1967 occupation of the Palestinian West Bank was equated to Turkey's 1974 occupation of northern Cyprus. On his first day in office, in April 1981, Papandreou invited Yasser Arafat to visit him in Athens. Subsequently, a PLO emissary shared with Israel's emissary the identical sub-ambassadorial status in the Greek capital. In the United Nations, as in the European Community, the Papandreou government functioned as the West's most dependable and uncompromising spokesman for the Palestinian cause. At Israel's invasion of Lebanon in June 1982, Papandreou called Israel a "murderer of women and children." Thereafter, some one hundred demonstrators converged on the Israeli diplomatic mission. The crowd was deterred from violence only by the presence of the United States embassy close by. In August the Papandreou government provided a flotilla of Greek vessels to evacuate PLO troops from Lebanon.

Papandreou's leftist PASOK government continued to vilify both Israel and the United States. Government agents organized public meetings on behalf of the PLO. PASOK newspapers denounced Moshe Gilboa, who arrived in Athens in 1986 as Israel's "diplomatic representative," as an American agent, and crowds periodically gathered outside his office shouting insults.

Nevertheless, Gilboa continued to focus his principal efforts on the Greek political opposition. In May 1988, he succeeded in organizing a visit to Israel by Constantine Mitsotakis and a bloc of New-Democratic parliamentarians. Mitsotakis then promised Gilboa that, if elected, he would seek to establish diplomatic relations with Israel. He kept his word. In the spring of 1990 the New-Democratic Party won a narrow second round electoral victory, and Mitsoutakis became prime minister. In the first session of parliament he requested approval for de jure recognition of Israel, and successfully pressed the issue through as a vote of confidence. Gilboa himself then submitted his credentials as Israel's first ambassador to Greece. For the Greek government and people, still deeply committed to the Palestinian cause, the new departure was less than a gesture of friendship to Israel. At best it signified an exercise in diplomatic realism.

Greece remained a choice killing ground. In July 1988, three Palestinians opened fire on a Greek cruise ship en route to Piraeus. Many of the passengers were Jews; nine were killed and forty-three wounded.

Britain

As early as the 1960s, the Mossad had developed a close relationship with British intelligence. With their own experience with IRA bombings, the British displayed little tolerance for terrorist atrocities of any kind. In continental Europe only West

German, Dutch, and Norwegian intelligence services provided Israel with comparable support.

In July 1987, a Palestinian attempted to blow up an El Al airliner by planting a bomb in the luggage of his pregnant Irish girlfriend. Thanks to an Israeli security guard, it was discovered in time at Heathrow Airport. In July 1988, Palestinians shot down an alleged Mossad informer in a London street. Subsequent police investigation revealed an extensive terrorist network in England, operating in numerous safe houses that functioned as ammunition cachés and laboratories for the manufacture of bombs and fake passports. Israel drew comfort from Britain's estimable record of cooperation in the struggle against terrorism.

CHAPTER SEVEN

The Oslo Accords

On the morning of April 12, 1988, Israel carried out its follow-up attack against PLO headquarters outside Tunis; Arafat's aid Wazir, known as Abu Jihad, was cut down in his villa.

In its lethal precision, the operation shook Arafat seriously. By then the PLO chairman had all but lost his underground war. He began scaling down his campaign. Another approach to the conflict would have to be explored.

In his book *The Process*, Uri Savir notes a change in attitude of the Palestinian leadership. He quotes Abu Ala, in 1992 in Oslo: "I believe we have arrived at the root of the problem. We have learned that our rejection of you will not bring us freedom. You can see that your control of us will not bring you security. We must live side by side in peace, equality and cooperation. This is also the view of our leadership in Tunis."

"We are interested in cooperating with you in all areas of life," Abu Ala stressed. "Naturally, we want our national rights and the liberty we deserve. But we realize this can be best enjoyed through cooperation with you, perhaps more than with any other neighbor."

On the Israeli side, the Right was defeated in the July 1992 elections and the Rabin government was inaugurated. In *Touching Peace*, Yossi Beillin called it a "dream government – Prime Minister Rabin and Foreign Minister Peres, while people who for years had been considered extreme left-wingers were serving as senior ministers.... The original idea was to revive something which had been tried and had failed before – to establish a secret track, solve the problems, conclude the process and, with the agreement of the leaderships on both sides, lay the completed work on the negotiating table without the existence of the track ever being known. To the world it would be seem that all the problems had been solved by official negotiation, while the truth would be very different...The declaration was presented as an agreement on mutual recognition with the PLO in which the Palestinians would attain self-government in exchange for cessation of terrorism, cooperation with Israel, and establishment of a basis of joint economic ventures."

The agreement included seven points:
1) Recognition of Israel's right to exist in security and peace.
2) Acceptance of Security Council Resolutions 242 and 338.
3) Resolution of the conflict by peaceful means.
4) Resolution of differences through negotiations.
5) Renunciation of terrorism.
6) Halt of the intifada.
7) Rescinding the clauses of the Palestinian Covenant that call for the destruction of Israel or otherwise contradict the peace process.

After Oslo, supporters of the peace process hoped that the PLO would be able to make the transition from an armed national liberation movement, deeply enmeshed in terrorism, into a responsible and viable political structure, ultimately leading to Palestinian sovereignty in a state living in peace alongside Israel.

The hope that Yasser Arafat could turn eventually into a Palestinian Nelson Mandela inspired even those Israelis who might have been skeptical about some aspects of the Oslo Accords.

But it was not to be. Arafat missed the historic opportunity of achieving a Palestinian state when he rejected a series of Barak-Clinton proposals at Camp David and Taba and instead unleashed terrorism and suicide attacks against Israeli civilian targets. The Palestinian territories themselves descended into a lawless chaos, which began the moment the Israeli government signed away Israel's heartland to a foreign terrorist entity's fifty-thousand-strong "police force," with rifles furnished by Israel. But the ultimate collapse of any "New Middle East" envisioned by Oslo's architects came in 1994, when the first buses with their scores of passengers exploded in downtown Jerusalem and Tel Aviv.

Writing in the *National Review* on June 12, 2002, historian Paul Johnson, whose books include *A History of the Jews*, claimed that the "Oslo Accords were a mistake and have been used by Arafat – and his foreign backers – merely as a platform from which to launch indiscriminate suicide bombings against Israel's cities. Ariel Sharon's walking on the Temple Mount was used by the Palestinian leaders as an excuse to scuttle a peace settlement they had never sincerely adhered to in the first place.

"For seven delusional years, we gorged ourselves on fat, farfetched fantasies. We fantasized that we could turn desperados into diplomats by dressing them in three-piece suits; we dreamt that we could secure a lasting peace by feeding the ravenous tiger, all the while ignoring his venomous nature and pledge to consume us. If the dream is now unmasked as the nightmare it truly is, we have only ourselves to blame for allowing it to happen – for helping it to happen – right under our very noses.

"Yet what matters most is not breast-beating or blame-laying; that can wait until the battle is ended. What matters now is that we do not repeat our tragic errors; that we fight the enemy with all our resources, and that we protect our citizens by eliminating – through any and every method – the merciless killers who seek our destruction."

In Column One of the *Jerusalem Post*, Thursday, May 16, 2001, Caroline B. Glick wrote that

"Oslo was based on the strategic assumption that the adoption of a conciliatory stance would benefit Israel diplomatically. The very notion that appeasing Palestinian aspirations would bring about international acceptance of Israel was literally blown to smithereens after Arafat reacted to Ehud Barak's unprecedented offers at Camp David by going to war. Rather than taking Israel's side, the international community has reacted to this situation by increasing its diplomatic isolation. Indeed, even the Bush administration, which is so outspokenly sympathetic, last November became the first US administration to openly support Palestinian statehood. Israeli openness and flexibility toward the Palestinians, far from bringing openness and diplomatic acceptance, have consistently fostered only greater diplomatic weakness and international isolation."

Barry Rubin in the *Jerusalem Post*, July 31, 2002:

"The eagerness of many European states to appease terrorists is a well-known phenomenon. In 1969, [officials in] the British Embassy in Amman began meeting secretly with a high ranking Fatah official authorized by Arafat for this purpose. This was at a time when Arafat was leader of PLO, an organization that included the PFELP, which was staging terror attacks in England.

"Rather than demand that Arafat do something to stop these activities, the British gave assurances that they bore no ill will toward Fatah for those facts, and expressed gratitude that Arafat had condemned them. The Foreign Ministry wanted to make it clear to Scotland Yard and to Immigration and Customs officers that if Fatah members were not treated properly, they might become angry. Another British diplomat urged the importance of good relations with Fatah and the PLO since they were 'one of the pillars of the state which may one day be a government.'

"One would never guess from this dialogue that, at the time, Fatah was staging terrorist attacks on Israelis; was a close ally of the PFELP; was subverting the Jordanian government, Britain's closest ally in the Middle East."

At the close of a meeting of the EU, the fifteen-member body issued a declaration on the Middle East that was both decidedly unbalanced and remarkably obtuse. That the EU is neither sympathetic nor favorable toward Israel hardly comes as a surprise. After all it has never shown itself to be a fair or balanced body when it comes to adjudicating the Arab-Israeli conflict. But what was really disappointing about the document was the willful delusion evident in it regarding Yasser Arafat and the PA. Indeed, by bestowing an unwarranted diplomatic prize on the PA, the EU has only served to encourage Arafat to continue his lethal obstinacy.

Although Arafat has done nothing to curb the rising tide of violence, the EU ministers persist in spreading the myth that he is a viable peace partner. In their declaration they said, "Israel needs the PA and its elected president, Yasser Arafat, as a partner to negotiate with, both in order to eradicate terrorism and to work toward peace. Their capacity to fight terrorism must not be weakened."

This statement is especially ludicrous in light of Fatah's open involvement in several deadly terror attacks, which hardly suggests they are suitable candidates to "eradicate terrorism." And the EU position is even more difficult to understand given that just two days before it was issued, Arafat gave a speech in Ramallah to a delegation from Hebron in which he said, "Yes, brothers, with our souls and blood we redeem you, O Palestine. This is the decision of the people; they said, 'God is great! Glory to God and his prophet! *Jihad, jihad, jihad, jihad, jihad!*'" That is hardly the rhetoric of a man interested in peace.

Even more preposterous was the EU's approach to the Karine A affair, in which Arafat was caught red-handed trying to smuggle illegal weapons from Iran. Despite overwhelming proof of his direct involvement, so compelling that it precipitated Washington's public change of tone vis-á-vis the PA, the EU fell for Arafat's transparent ploy of establishing a commission of inquiry to investigate the matter. In its declaration, the EU "urges the speedy completion of the work of the investigative commission established by the PA to clarify the circumstances of the Karine A affair. The EU would also welcome international involvement in the work of the commission." And so, the EU made itself an active partner in Arafat's little charade, allowing him to continue to assert with a straight face, no less, that he had nothing to do with the smuggling operation.

Of course, when it comes to Israel, the EU ministers were far less inclined to give Prime Minister Ariel Sharon the benefit of the doubt. Rather than expressing support for Israel in its battle against Palestinian terror, the EU chose to sharply criticize the government: "Withdraw its military forces, stop the extra-judicial executions, lift the closures and all the restrictions imposed on the Palestinian people and its leadership, and freeze the settlements." The EU ministers even had the gall to suggest Israel should pay reparations for having damaged EU-financed infrastructure projects such as Gaza International Airport.

The EU statement came just days after US President George Bush expressed his public disappointment with Arafat and even accused him of "enhancing terrorism." By breaking with the American position, the Europeans have regrettably chosen to undermine the diplomatic isolation and international pressure brought to bear on Arafat recently. In doing so, they have sent a dangerous message to the Palestinians that they can continue to act with impunity. Though the EU ministers did urge Arafat to act against terrorism, such pleas are unlikely to move him, if only because he knows the brunt of European criticism remains directed at Israel.

Under the title *Hooligans Take Their Cue*, Evelyn Gordon wrote in the *Jerusalem Post* on Tuesday, May 14, 2002:

"The European Union is outraged. Javier Solana, the EU's foreign policy chief, gave a speech last Thursday lambasting the American media for accusing Europe of anti-Semitism. Such accusations, he said, are 'deeply unjust,' 'of striking brutality,' and 'don't correspond to reality.' Two days earlier the EU's commissioner for external relations, Chris Patten, published a similar diatribe in the *Washington Post*, terming such charges 'obscenely offensive rubbish,' and a 'mad and grotesque assault on reasoned debate.' And both of them reiterated the standard defenses: Not all criticism of Israel is anti-Semitic, anti-Jewish violence in Europe is 'imported' from the Middle East. The government is not responsible for every hooligan who vandalizes a synagogue. European governments always denounce such attacks.

"But all of these justifications, though true, fail to explain the one salient fact that Patten and Solana carefully avoided mentioning: while anti-Semitic violence is up sharply in Europe, there has been no similar upsurge in the United States.

"Like Europe, the US has a large Moslem community that cares deeply about the Middle East. It also has a very visible Jewish community that would provide an easy target for anti-Semitic attacks. Yet according to the Anti-Defamation League, the US has experienced no increase at all in anti-Semitic incidents over the last nineteen months. So why do American Moslems confine themselves to democratic protest – demonstrations, lobbying, articles in the press – while European Moslems add synagogue vandalism and assault on Jewish schoolchildren to their repertoire? Is it just chance that all the hooligans are in Europe? Discounting this far-fetched thesis, the unavoidable conclusion is that Europe has somehow created a climate conducive to anti-Semitic violence, while the US has not. And if one compares the American media, government, and public to their European counterparts, the 'how' is easy to see.

"The mainstream American media, like its European counterpart, is highly critical of Israel. Nevertheless, there are some key differences. The American press, for instance, does not inflame its readers with classic anti-Semitic cartoons – like the one in the respected Italian paper *La Stampa*, in which baby Jesus peers up at an Israeli tank and says: 'Don't tell me they want to kill me again!'"

Perhaps even more importantly, the American media does not obscure such crucial facts as that the IDF operations it so deplores are responses to suicide bombings targeting Israeli civilians. That is not true in Europe – as Jan Daniel, editor of the French weekly *Le Nouvel Observateur* noted in a scathing editorial in February. Daniel, incidentally, is hardly an Israel-lover: in December, he rushed to publish an unverified front page story accusing Israeli soldiers of raping Palestinian women (he later had to retract it). Yet by February, even he was appalled by the French media's "unprofessionalism." "The media," he wrote, "simply ignores the terror attacks that precede Israeli military actions. Day after day, they lead the reader to conclude that Israeli troops are killing Palestinians for no reason at all."

By portraying Israelis (read "Jews") as people who kill without cause, the media creates a climate for anti-Semitic violence. Psychopathic killers do not deserve the protections accorded ordinary human beings.

The broader American public also behaves differently from its European counterpart. There is no lack of support for the Palestinian cause in the US. Witness the number of non-Moslems attending pro-Palestinian rallies. But you would never find American trade unionists parading in Hamas garb, as Italy's trade unionists did, not long ago. Such actions, again, send the implicit message that violence against Jews is acceptable: Since Hamas is the inventor of suicide bombings against Israeli women and children, if its members are heroes worth emulating, then killing Jews must be right and proper.

And finally, there are the governments. The Bush administration is hardly uncritical of Israel: It is the first American government to speak of a Palestinian state and

Israel's "occupation of Palestine," and it regularly urges military restraint. Yet it also acknowledges that governments must defend their citizens against terrorism, and therefore not every Israeli military action is automatically wrong.

Though European governments also pay lip service to Israel's right of self-defense, in nearly two years of conflict there is not a single Israeli tactic that they have not unequivocally condemned.

Closures are wrong and roadblocks are wrong, bombing is wrong and ground operations are wrong, even returning fire when shot is wrong. The underlying message is clear: In reality Israel has no right to self-defense – the only country in the world so circumscribed. And if Israel alone has no right to defend its citizens, then attacks on those citizens must be justified.

European hooligans have in fact grasped perfectly the real message being broadcast by their governments, public, and media: that anti-Jewish violence is "understandable." And as long as this is so, no amount of official condemnation of such attacks can absolve Europe of the charge of anti-Semitism.

Ovadia Sofer wrote in The *Jerusalem Post* on August 4, 2002:

> "Europe, for its part and as usual, is straining to differentiate itself from American policy. The EC, which currently maintains the West's main link with Palestinian leader Yasser Arafat and his men, is consciously sabotaging the Bush administration's policy of effecting real change in the Palestinian leadership.

> "European support of Arafat has led to a toughening in Palestinian positions, forcing the Bush admini-

stration to make concessions such as the American agreement to entrust the future of the regional peace process to the 'quartet,' including the Europeans, the Russians and the UN.

Based on past experience, these countries have been obstacles more than facilitators. In addition to their ties with Arafat, European representatives in Israel claim that they are the main party mediating a dialogue between the PA and the Hamas leadership with the aim of achieving an end to suicide attacks in Israel. These efforts accelerated following the liquidation of arch-terrorist Salah Shehadeh.

"As far as Israel is concerned, the EU's test will be the degree to which it supports the American demand to include the condemnation of the terrorist organizations, by name, in any future resolution proposal on the Middle East conflict submitted to the UN Security Council, which the Arab bloc has turned into the main tool in its conflict with Israel.

"The significance of all this diplomatic activity is not so much in what it might accomplish, but rather in what it might prevent. The more European and Arab diplomats attempt to rearrange the deck chairs of the current system, the more the Bush administration's revolutionary concepts, such as a regime change, and Arab democratization, seem to fade into the distance."

Douglas Davis, London correspondent of the GP, in the *Jerusalem Post*, July, 2002:

"The EU seems ever ready to appease rogue states when presented with the prospect of 'trade opportunities.' Just one week before President George W. Bush declared the Palestinian leadership to be tainted by terrorism, the EU was cranking out a series of petticoat-revealing decisions, demonstrating once again its selective and cynical approach to terrorists."

Poking a finger in the eye of its transatlantic ally, which regards Iran as a founding member of the "axis of evil," Europe announced it was intensifying its pursuit of the Islamic Republic. In a ground-breaking declaration, the EU's foreign ministers solemnly resolved to "fast-track" political and trade talks with Iran, while demanding, Canute-like, that it cease terrorist activities and abandon its non-conventional weapons programs. Never mind Iran's bloody calls for the destruction of Israel, and its implacable opposition to any diplomatic accommodation with the "Little Satan;" never mind its demonstrable support for terrorism and its feverish request to acquire nuclear weapons.

The EU's External Relations Commissioner, Chris Patten, appears to harbor the bizarre expectation that Europe's "hand of friendship" will serve as an optical corrective, encouraging the mullahs to see the virtue of moderation and reform. But the EU's foreign ministers were not content with a simple declaration of friendship to mark their collective discourse with despotic, oil-rich Moslem states; in the case of Iran, a regime that would be regarded as a threat and treated as a pariah if it existed within missile range of mainland Europe.

In reviewing its blacklist of terror organizations which was inspired by September 11, the EU foreign ministers conspicuously omitted one of the most notorious of all international terrorist groups, which is armed, equipped, trained, and financed by Iran.

The omission is an indication of the depths of Europe's appeasement and duplicity. At the same time, the European parliament resumed its habit of suspending disbelief when it decided on continued financial aid for the PA after assurances from the ubiquitous Patten that no EU money had been used to fund terrorism, despite concrete evidence to the contrary.

In preceding weeks, the EU – second only to the Arab states as a benefactor to the Palestinians – received damning Israeli evidence that proved Arafat's personal authorization for payments to terrorists and their families. The Europeans also had access to a major investigation published by the respected German daily *Die Zeit*, which flatly stated: "Brussels is ignoring what the PLO chief is doing with his EU funds." Everywhere it looked, the newspaper found that "EU funds which were intended to promote peace were used for making war, and funds intended for the construction of democratic structures were used to finance the terror network."

The result of the investigation, noted the paper, are "alarming."

While Patten chose to ignore the evidence, he might have tuned in to the PA's television station, underwritten by the EU, to see how Europe's largesse is being used.

When the reporters of *Die Zeit* did just that, they found the station waging an eternal war against the Jews, explaining "Allah's war of liquidation of the state of Israel."

And when a Belgian deputy, Oliver Dupuis, asked whether the EU Commission "considers it acceptable that EU funding is being used to foster hatred toward the Israeli people, Patten responded disingenuously that the EU's agreement with the PA is based on the "respect of democratic principles and fundamental human rights." Nor does the EU shy away from contributing handsomely toward a Palestinian education system whose textbooks propagate anti-Semitism, eulogizing suicide "martyrs" and denying Israel's existence on its maps in states of the region.

Die Zeit concluded that the cumulative evidence indicates that "Arafat and his people used donations from foreign countries, including the EU, to finance their terrorism."

Patten however, remained defiant: "The EU Commission has to date not been shown any hard evidence that EU funds have been misused to finance terrorism, or any other purpose."

The Dutch daily *NRC Handelsblad* quoted diplomats in Brussels as saying that the EU had deliberately refrained from monitoring the Palestinians' use of European aid to finance terrorism and corruption, "because it feared this would jeopardize the resumption of the Middle East peace process."

More than half of all the EU's foreign aid is directed at the Palestinian Authority. Between 1994 and 2001, according to the *NRC Handelsblad*, the EU delivered 1,446 billion euros in aid to the Palestinians, including 256 million euros in loans from the European Investment Bank. Individual member states kicked in a further one billion euros to the PA coffers. By any reckoning, some of that must have found its way to Iran to pay for the consignment of rockets, grenades, anti-tank weapons, machine guns, mines and twenty-two hundred kilograms of explosive that were seized by Israel while en route from Teheran to the Gaza Strip on board the Karine A.

However, the prize for *hutzpa* must go to Arafat's all-purpose aide Nabi Sha'ath, who confronted members of the EC at their Valencia conference in April with a demand for no less than 1.9 billion dollars in aid. Among the items in his shopping list was 20.6 million dollars for weapons and 40.6 million for the support of refugees and "martyr families."

In the words of *Die Zeit*, the assembled diplomats "did not greet this demand with alarm, they were not horrified, only embarrassed. They let the wish list disappear into the vault. They did not want to know anything about it. They would rather be defrauded discreetly."

European Commission's Response

Giancarlo Chevallard, European Union head of the European Commission Delegation to the State of Israel, in the *Jerusalem Post*, on August 4, 2002:

"On July 11, the *Jerusalem Post* published an opinion by Attorney Leitner on the sensitive issue of EU funding to the Palestinians under the title *Brussels' Wartime Profiteers*.

"What Leitner omitted to indicate was the fact that she represents plaintiffs in a claim submitted to the District Court in Tel Aviv which is founded on basically the same accusations and allegations stated in her article. In this respect, her article seems to be designated to form a pre-trial public opinion supporting the claim submitted by her to the court.

"The EU has full confidence in the Israeli judiciary system and will not take part in any unethical attempt to try the case in the press. I will therefore simply reiterate some basic facts."

I consider it sufficient to say that the harsh allegations stated in Leitner's article are shameful and baseless. The EU does not fund terrorism. The EU assistance to the Palestinians is directed to support humanitarian interventions, assistance to refugees through UNRWA, development projects in infrastructures, technical assistance, Israeli-Arab-Palestinian cooperation initiatives at civil society level, budgetary assistance and loans to the private sector. The budgetary assistance to the PA is a recent development and represents a small part of the EU support.

"The EU has taken the lead, in the last decade, in promoting Palestinian economic development and the emergence of effective and accountable institutions as a contribution to the peace process. The EU, and other donors, like Japan, Canada, Norway, and many Arab countries have decided since the beginning of this intifada to take on themselves the burden of financing the PA budget, with the purpose of ensuring that basic services in the fields of health, education, social services and public order continue to be provided to the Palestinian population. Such aid is believed to reduce the risk that increasing misery, anarchy and unemployment would lead to more Palestinian anger and violence against Israelis.

"At the same time, the EU and other participating states have successfully exerted leverage on the PA leadership for better and more transparent management while pressing for basic reforms in its governance and administration. The EU will continue to fund these causes and Commissioner Patten, supported by EU member states and the European parliament, has made this point forcefully.

"The EU exercises control of the use of its funds, and all budgetary assistance is strictly vetted."

Payments are only transferred after the International Monetary Fund has verified that the money has been properly spent according to the agreed purpose. I find it disgraceful that the article discredits the IMF, and its local director's work.

"Disagreements and criticism between Israelis and Europeans on EU policies (and vice versa) are a normal part of our healthy bilateral relationship. Their value and credibility would be reinforced if they were not based on distortions of facts, unsubstantiated allegations, misrepresentations of motives and personal attacks."

On July 28, 2002, Education Minister Limor Livnat wrote Anders Fogh Rasmussen, Prime Minister of Denmark and EU president, voicing her concern over the perversion of history and anti-Israel propaganda in Palestinian textbooks:

"Your Excellency,

"First I would like to take this opportunity to congratulate you on your assumption of the presidency of the European Union. I wish you much success in all your endeavors. In addition, I admire greatly your courageous stand in joining President George W. Bush's call for the replacement of the present Palestinian leadership, i.e. Arafat and his coterie. Their stewardship of the Palestinian Authority has not contributed to the peace process.

"A serious issue regarding the present Palestinian leadership is that of textbooks in the PA. Last year European parliament member and French lawyer Francois Zimeray brought to the world community's attention the problem of what the PA education system teaches its students. He stated that while he does not oppose EU funding of the education system, that system should be promoting peace, not indoctrinating its youth to hatred and to turning themselves into human bombs.

"Progress has been made somewhat with the amendment to the EU budget last year.

"Budget line B7-42 allocates approximately 45 million euros for programs promoting peace in the Middle East, including textbooks and other educational activity in the PA. The amendment to this line states that 'money should not be used for activities, projects and programs that promote principles or opinions that are not consistent with the basic values of the European Union, only for projects that support peace, understanding, reconciliation and a decrease of hate.' The accompanying explanatory note forbids EU money to be used in support of textbooks that include racism and anti-Semitism.

"We welcome this small step and urge the EU to encourage its member states, who provide the PA education system with money through bilateral agreements, to take similar action.

"However, the facts on the ground show that the PA is not using those funds as intended. The Center Monitoring the Impact of Peace in its latest survey released in November 2001 shows that in the fifty-eight books it reviewed, the concept of peace with Israel is not to be found. Israel is referred to as the lands within the Green Line. Palestine is considered to be all the territory between the Jordan River and the Mediterranean Sea. Jerusalem belongs only to the Palestinians. Jewish holy sights do not exist; on the contrary, there are only Moslem and Christian sites in Jerusalem, despite Israel's attempt to 'judaize' the city.

"PA textbooks have perverted history. For example, there is minimal mention of the Jewish historical connection to the Land of Israel, nor is there any attempt to provide basic knowledge of Jews or Judaism. The Western Wall, the only remnant of Judaism's Temple, destroyed in 587 BCE and again in 70 CE, and its holiest site – is referred to as the al-Burak wall. Maps of Palestine shown in the most up-to-date textbooks refer to what is in fact all of Israel and the territories.

"Reference is made to the tragic fire set in 1969 by a mentally ill Christian Australian tourist. However, in the version of National Education Grade 7 page 55 the incident refers to (Israeli) attempts at obliterating the artistic (Palestinian) heritage by setting fire to the antique pulpit of Saladin in the al Aksa Mosque.

"In National Education grade 2 part 1 (2001), page 4 there is a blatant and purposeful error when it states that the Canaanite Arabs were the first ones who settled in Palestine. Jews are referred to pejoratively as greedy, barbaric and tricky. This is hardly in the spirit of the EU budget or in the spirit of the Oslo Accords, which have been buried by the present Palestinian war of terror against Israel.

"As I told the UNESCO General Conference in Paris on October 18, 2001: Terrorism does not begin with the hijacking of a plane, or strapping oneself with explosives, or the indiscriminate shooting in a crowd of people, or into a school bus. Terrorism begins with education, that is, education for hatred.

"It is the cultivation of unbridled hatred that breeds unrestrained terrorism. The suicide bombers who have claimed the lives of hundreds of innocent people in my country, including teachers and schoolchildren, were taught from the cradle.

"This fanaticism is ever present in the PA's new textbooks, not to mention its old ones. A few examples:

'There is no alternative to destroying Israel.'

'The Jewish goal is to establish a global Jewish empire whose territory will be not only from the Nile to the

Euphrates, and from Medina to Kuwait – the true goal of the Jews is to rob the Arabs of their homeland.'

'Jihad comes first after worship.'

'Our dear students, may peace come upon you and God's mercy and blessings. We expect you – after learning the unit 'Lord of the Martyrs,' about the first Moslem martyr – to realize the glorification of the concept of martyrdom and martyrs.'

"A seventh-grade assignment is to 'mention the names of Palestinian and Arab jihad fighters who fell as martyrs while defending Palestine.'

"The CMIP report is replete with further evidence with the PA's indoctrination of hatred against Jews and Israel in its education system.

"Mr. Prime Minister, as Israel's minister of education, I beseech you to use your moral authority and power of the purse, especially now in your new position as president of the European Union, to end this propaganda which leads, and has led, to the death of hundreds of Israelis, including schoolchildren. It is no coincidence that it was precisely in the chapter on the training of children in Plutarch's *Morals* that he wrote: 'Words are but the shadow of actions.'

"I thank you for your serious consideration in this matter.

Sincerely,

Limor Livnat"

The minister of education received a reply on September 25, 2002:

"Your Excellency,

"Thank you for your letter and for your kind words concerning my assumption of the presidency of the European Union.

"In your letter you express concern over textbooks presently in use in the Palestinian education system, with reference to an enclosed survey made by the Center for Monitoring the Impact of Peace in November 2001. I fully agree with you that fanaticism and incitement have no place in educational material. I therefore find the quotations in your letter from the new textbooks highly disturbing.

"According to information gathered by the EU mission as well as independent studies carried out by Israelis and Palestinians, academics and educators, the allegations against the new textbooks should be unjustified. The studies show that whereas a number of quotations attributed to the new textbooks in the Center for Monitoring the Impact on Peace report of November 2001 could be confirmed, these have been badly translated or quoted out of context, thus suggesting an anti-Jewish bias or incitement that the books do not contain.

"According to the said studies, the textbooks should be free of incitement content. The new textbooks should thus represent an improvement over previous textbooks. Likewise an assessment from the George Eckert Institute for International Textbook Research states, among other things, that the 'new textbooks – in contrast to the old Jordanian and Egyptian ones – no longer contain any of the prejudices generally derogatory to the Jews or Israelis, or anti-Semitic stereotypes.'

"This said, I do find the quotations in your letter from the new textbooks highly disturbing and I will take steps to insure that the matter is looked into and addressed. You can therefore expect the Danish Ministry of Foreign Affairs to contact Israeli authorities in order to look into the matter.

"Let me assure you that we will address the issue with an open mind and with great seriousness.

"Yours sincerely,

"Anders Fogh Rasmussen"

What Europe has to Offer

Marc Daugherty, a Tel Aviv-based European affairs analyst, in the *Jerusalem Post* of Sunday, May 19, 2002:

"Bravo to the EU's ambassador to Israel, Giancarlo Chevallard, for his recent observation: 'The potential of our overall relationship is not fully appreciated. Europe and Israel can and must do better.' The Middle East is one place where the Europeans are eager to translate their economic weight into political influence. Indeed the European Union has recently portrayed itself as a 'new superpower.' In EU President Romano Prodi's terms, it should stand equal with the United States.

"And yet, amid palpably decaying EU-Israel ties, it is high time Europe's leaders ponder why their policies in the region are so firmly set on a road to nowhere.

"The EU's willingness to be more active in the peace process, so important for Europe's stability, is widely viewed in Israel with suspicion. No wonder. Since the start of the current intifada, Israelis keep wondering why the EU appears to do its best to stick to a pattern of egregious one-sided steps. For months Israelis had to bear European pronouncements decrying Israeli defensive actions as if they reflected some inscrutable caprice.

"Later, Spain proceeded to start its EU presidency with a demand that Israel compensate the EU for damages inflicted on European-funded PA infrastructure. Interestingly the EU Parliament then threatened to slap Israel with severe sanctions should it refuse to accept European mediation.

"Europe's foreign policy must not be driven by the mere urge for recognition. Europe had better tempt Israel with a carrot, not beat it so compulsively with a stick. Its isolation of Israel has proven hugely counterproductive – not unlike Israel's high profile military siege on Arafat, which has made him more popular than ever.

"Contrary to Continental common wisdom, Israelis have not lost faith in the ideal of peace. Rather, they have lost hope in the vision originally set out in Oslo, the idea that the Arabs would accept Israel as an equal partner in some sort of open Middle East common market. It is now clear that is not going to happen any time soon, the Saudi plan notwithstanding.

"Until now, no substitute vision has been put on the table, perhaps so that Europe can contribute both to Israel and the Arab Middle East. After World War II, the French and Germans were associated with Italy and the Benelux to achieve lasting peace on the continent. Along these lines Europe should associate with Israel to achieve peace, an idea ironically supported by no fewer than forty-three members of the European parliament.

"To achieve superpower status, Europe need not send off aircraft carriers to the four corners of the globe. The Europeans have invented a new system of international governance with freedom and prosperity as its basis. Europe is already a superpower – a superpower of democratic ideas. As such, it must further move to reassess its cherished policy of holding on to Yasser Arafat at all cost, no matter how repressive his regime. It is now clear that PA corruption and widespread human rights abuses have all but fed the Palestinians' sense that peace with Israel could be no more legitimate than the dictatorship forced upon them.

"For better or worse, Europe has become the Palestinians' strategic ally in the same manner that the US is vital to Israel. Europe is ideally placed to provide Palestinians with the support and incentives to become the Arab world's first democracy. Sadly, as EU published figures show, European aid for Palestinian human rights and democracy projects accounts for a meager one third of one percent of the approximate 800 million dollars doled out to the PA since 2000. This is in contrast with Israel's free trade agreement with the EU, which requires strict adherence to human rights. Surely Europe does not believe democracy is not for the Palestinians.

"Europe created the Middle East conflict as a result of anti-Semitism and colonialism. Now it should have the courage to be part of the solution – two independent democracies – living side by side in peace and security."

Robert S. Wistrich, professor of European History at the Hebrew University of Jerusalem, writes under the title *Europe and the Moslem War Against the Jews*:

"The rising tide of anti-Semitic vitriol across Europe – with synagogues burning in Paris, London and Marseilles, and the old pogrom's cry of 'death to the Jews!' once more echoing from Brussels to Kiev – has shocked many in Israel and the Diaspora. Such hostility has not been seen since the end of World War II and has exposed the dormant genocidal demons still lurking beneath the civilized veneer of Europe, as well as the hollowness of its pretension to moral superiority. Much less attention has been paid, however, to the massive Moslem contribution to this wave of anti-Semitism, which in Europe and the West has found its most enthusiastic supporters among recent Arab and Moslem immigrants. Since October 2000 there has been an alarming rise in the number of anti-Semitic assaults on Jewish communities around the world for which young Moslems have been responsible, and nowhere is this more apparent than in France. These new immigrants carry with them anti-Semitic baggage from their mother countries and Islamic culture.

"Their hatred is further reinforced by the malevolently Judeophobic sermons heard in their local mosques or the scenes of 'martyrdom' continually relayed by satellite TV programs from the Middle East. This highly explosive cocktail of fanatical religious passion, Jew-hatred and war-like zeal, sometimes perfectly encapsulated in the concept of Jihad (holy war), has been still further inflamed by the violently anti-Israel coverage of the Palestinian intifada in most of the French and the European media.

"Not only that, but the Moslem war against the Jews, especially in Europe, is also fuelled by their feelings of alienation, exclusion and marginalization, largely the product of an unsuccessful integration into the majority culture. Many Moslems see themselves as victims of European racism and displace their rage against the far more successful Jews whose influence they tend to exaggerate. Their frustrations and resentment have led to an intense though vicarious identification with the 'Palestinian victims of Israeli aggression.' Meanwhile, the Jews, particularly in France, with the growing specter of Le Pen adding fuel to the flames, find themselves caught between the new Islamic Judeophobia, the anti-Arab xenophobia (tinged with anti-Semitism) of the Front National and the Israelphobia of much of the European mass media.

"One of the paradoxes of the present situation is that only with the electoral success of Le Pen have the Western media begun to acknowledge (though somewhat grudgingly) that anti-Semitism is indeed a problem, though whenever possible it is subordinated to the wider issue of racism. But when it comes to Moslem anti-Semitism, the West inexplicably looks the other way. The ubiquity of Moslem incitement against Jews, from Cairo to Damascus, Baghdad, Teheran, and Lahore is barely commented upon. Its direct connection to the terrorist war of the Islamists against Israel and the West is underplayed, if it is mentioned at all. Even the deluge of venomous Judeophobia widely available in Arab and Moslem bookshops and on video cassettes in Europe itself is rarely investigated though it clearly amounts to a culture of incitement. Holocaust denial material, when sponsored, promoted, or disseminated by Moslems, arouses only a ripple of interest. Yet the same phenomenon when it can be linked to Neo-Nazis or Neo-Fascists is most extensively covered by the Western media.

"Another virtually taboo subject is the close resemblance between Nazi and Italian anti-Semitism. This is apparent in the visual imagery of the Arab press, which endlessly indulges in hideous stereotype of Jews reminiscent of the classic Nazi propaganda rag *Der Stürmer*. Moslems have largely taken over the Nazi conspiratorial view of world Jewry as a giant octopus controlling the world's wealth and mass media, manipulating the US, fomenting wars and revolutions, and seeking to dominate the planet by subverting all rivals – especially Islam. Israel, in particular, is portrayed as the incarnation of evil, populated by criminal racists and Shylocks in military uniform, whose policies include spreading drugs, vice, prostitution, AIDS and the cultural poisons of modernity into Moslem society. From there it is but a small leap to embracing the idea that all the Jews of Israel should be eliminated. Hence the widespread glorification among Palestinians, Arabs and millions of Moslems of the suicide bombers who deliberately target innocent Israeli civilians. But to discuss these causes and effects would, it appears, be most inconvenient to the good conscience of many self-righteous Europeans. After all, only sixty years ago the unquenchable hatred we are now seeing on the Moslem street was also rampant among the peoples of Europe whose complicity and in many cases active collaboration made the Nazi extermination of Jews possible.

"But the impeccably 'anti-racist' and humanist Europeans of today prefer not to recognize their handiwork in the perverted and genocidal ideology of Islamist anti-Semitism, for which historically they bear considerable guilt.

"Instead they stand by almost silently when they are not actively denying the existence of Moslem Jew baiting or trying to excuse it as a purely political act of 'resisting the occupation.' This trivializing response to the Moslem war against the Jews (which has its counterparts in Israel and the Diaspora) reminds me of the failure of the West to effectively counter Nazi anti-Semitism. It smacks of appeasement, cowardice, and a failure to confront Europe's inner demons, which have instead been projected with almost hysterical fury against the alleged sins of the Jewish State. But the original sin of European racism will not be so easily exorcised, and deflecting it against Israel is likely to prove as suicidal as the exploding bombers who are wrecking the Palestinian cause."

Europe's duplicity

The recent almost comic mini-clash between Spain and Morocco over a tiny islet claimed by both countries brings into focus some difficult dilemmas faced by Spanish foreign policy. At a time when Spain presses its claims for the end of British colonial rule over Gibraltar, it appears that Spanish foreign policy is plagued by some of the nationalistic legacies of the Franco dictatorship.

Spain has a case against Britain regarding Gibraltar, which Spain lost in the 1713 Peace of Utrecht. Yet it is the case that over the almost three hundred years of British rule on the Rock, a population has evolved there which is mainly not of Spanish descent, does not speak Spanish, and does not view itself as part of the Spanish nation.

The elected chief minister of Gibraltar, Peter Caruana, certainly speaks for a universally accepted principle of European and democratic politics when he says that it is inconceivable that Britain and Spain decide on the future of Gibraltar without consulting with its population. Spain, however, utterly denies the right of the population of Gibraltar to decide on its future through a plebiscite, referendum, or any other means.

It appears that Spanish political thinking still maintains that a territory overrides the right of a population for self-determination. Spain calls for the right of self-determination for the Palestinians, regardless of Jewish historical and political claims to the West Bank, or even Jerusalem, but when it comes to its own claims, territory appears to be sacred and historical rights seem to take precedence over self-determination.

There is even a more troubling aspect in Spain's position: Spain controls two enclaves – Ceuta and Melilla – on the northern coast of Morocco, occupied by Spain several centuries ago. By all universally accepted criteria, these two cities should be part of Morocco. Spain's right of conquest surely cannot hold in the 21st century. Yet Spain finds no problem in claiming

Gibraltar while denying the same right to Morocco over Ceuta and Melilla.

If the EU cannot enforce principles of self-determination and equal justice on its own members, how can it preach to others?

Sol Liebgott, a governor of the Hebrew University, writing in the *Jerusalem Post* in July, 2002:

> "Norway is the nation that gave the world the word *quisling*, after Vidkun Quisling, the Norwegian politician who encouraged the Nazi invasion of his country. Norwegians are not proud of this contribution to the English language, but they should be at least as disturbed by their leadership role in the anti-Israel wave that is sweeping Europe.

> "On the heels of UN Mid East representative Terje Larsen's now infamous remark that 'Israel ceded all moral ground in Jenin,' comes word from his home country of Norway that some supermarket chains have decided to place special identification stickers on products from Israel. Other Scandinavian countries may follow suit. The Norwegians say that stickers do not constitute a boycott of Israel; they just want their customers, who are overwhelmingly pro-Palestinian, to note where these products are produced. Maybe the rest of us should run down to the supermarkets with a pad of yellow stickers so that customers of Norwegian salmon or Norwegian cheese can also pay attention to the source of these products – a source with a shameful past that continues to operate as a

European free zone for Neo-Nazi and other right wing extremists.

"Those asking the question whether Europeans are anti-Israel because of Israel's action in fighting terror, or because of their own latent anti-Semitism, should study the examples of Norway. Behind the current disclaimer of a boycott you will find that Norwegians are quite experienced at shunning Israel. Norwegian labor unions have recently refused to offload Israel farm produce. Last year a Norwegian youth movement organized a campaign to ban Israeli singers from the Eurovision song contest. Another Norwegian group was boycotting Israeli oranges since the early '90s. This group "*Boikott Israel*," rejuvenated by the latest intifada to include a boycott of all Israeli commerce, denies on its web site that it is anti-Semitic but states that the goal is to end Israel's 'fifty year occupation of, and the return of all refugees, to a free Palestine.' Not anti-Semitic? In 1941, the graffiti on Jewish businesses in Oslo read 'Jews go to Palestine.' To campaign now in Norway to get the Jews out of Palestine by a process of elimination certainly bears the stamp of anti-Semitism.

"Indeed, the roots of Norwegian boycotts of Israel run deep. Anti-Semitism has held a unique place in Norwegian politics since the 1930s, when the same Vidkun Quisling, later the leader of a Nazi puppet government in Norway, formed the National Union Party. While many Norwegians fought with the resistance, many became eager collaborators of the Nazis, including some sixty thousand members of the National Union. Under its auspices, Norway formed its own branch of the SS and established academies sending hundreds of officers each year to the German military. One very active neo-Nazi group in Norway is the Institute for the History of Occupied Norway, composed of descendants of members of the Quisling party, the Waffen SS and others dedicated to cleansing their wartime reputation.

"The aspect of the Holocaust in Norway that was particularly Norwegian was the liquidation of Jewish property, much of which was divided up between Quisling and his followers. When the war ended, the Norwegian commission for reparations shamelessly accepted doctored figures kept by the Quisling government in order to reject most Jewish claims and avoid paying others more than pennies on the dollar. Then in 1997 a new commission issued a report that actually recommended adherence to the earlier decision. A scandal, however, erupted when it was discovered that an organization of former Nazis had provided a scholarship to a researcher on the new commission. The Norwegian Prime Minister intervened and compelled the government to accept a dissenting report.

"Today, neo-Nazi propaganda, including concerts and other events, are commonplace in Norway and the extreme right-wing Progress Party is the second largest party in Norway, with twenty-five out of hundred and sixty seats in parliament. Among other racist and anti-immigration views, this party advocates banning male circumcision. Kosher slaughter has already been forbidden by Norwegian law."

In 1994 the Nobel committee in Norway awarded its peace prize to Yitzhak Rabin, Shimon Peres, and Yasser Arafat. At that time, the honest member of the committee, Kaare Kristiansen, resigned in protest, calling Arafat a terrorist unworthy of the award. Now, however, other members, one of them a Lutheran Bishop, said they wanted to strip not Arafat but Shimon Peres, the most dovish minister in Israel's government, of the prize.

"But this is not all. The leader of the Socialist Left party also demanded reparations from Israel for destroying Palestinian infrastructure paid for by Norwegian aid money; that this aid money subsidized the shelter of armed terrorists and their activities seems of little concern to Norway."

Given their past and present history, Norwegians are hardly qualified to accuse any other country of having ceded moral ground. Their warning stickers of Israeli goods are the modern day equivalent of painting *Yoden* on the Jewish-owned businesses of Oslo and Trondheim in 1941. We need not be reminded that almost all of the Norway's Jews were deported to Auschwitz. Fewer than thirty survived the Holocaust.

"There seems ample reason not to buy Norwegian products any time soon or cruising on the Norwegian Line."

The Arafat I Know, by Ion Mihai Pacepa

General Pacepa was the highest ranking intelligence officer ever to have defected from the former Soviet bloc. His account of relations with Yasser Arafat was published in the *Wall Street Journal* on January 11, 2002:

"Last week, Israel seized a boat carrying fifty tons of Iranian-made mortars, long range missiles, and anti-tank rockets destined for the Palestinian Authority. The vessel, Karine A, is owned by the PA and its captain and several crew are members of the Palestinian naval police. I am not surprised to see that Yasser Arafat remains the same bloody terrorist I knew so well during my years at the top of Romania's foreign intelligence service.

"I became directly involved with Arafat in the late '60s, in the days when he was being financed and manipulated by the KGB. In the 1967 Six Day War, Israel humiliated two of the Soviet Union's Arab client states, Egypt and Syria. A couple of months later, the head of Soviet foreign intelligence, Gen. Alexander Sakharovsky, landed in Bucharest. According to him, the Kremlin had charged the KGB to 'repair the prestige of our Arab friends' by helping them organize terrorist operations that would humiliate Israel. The main KGB asset in this joint venture was a 'devoted Marxist-Leninist,' Yasser Arafat, co-founder of Fatah, the Palestinian military force."

Gen. Sakharovsky asked us in Romanian intelligence to help the KGB bringing Arafat and some of his Fedayeen fighters secretly to the Soviet Union via Romania, in order for them to be indoctrinated and trained. During that same year, the Soviets maneuvered to have Arafat named the chairman of the PLO with public help from Egypt's ruler Gamal Abd al-Nasser.

> "When I first met Arafat, I was stunned by the ideological similarity between him and his KGB mentor. Arafat's broken record was that American 'imperial Zionism' was the 'rabid dog of the world,' and there was only one way to deal with a rabid dog: 'Kill it!' In the years when Gen. Sakharovsky was the chief Soviet intelligence adviser in Romania, he used to preach in his soft melodious voice that the 'bourgeoisie was the rabid dog of imperialism,' adding that there was 'just one way to deal with a rabid dog: Shoot it!' He was responsible for killing fifty thousand Romanians.

> "In 1972, the Kremlin established a socialist division of labor for supporting international terrorism. Romania's main clients in this new market were Libya and the PLO. A year later, a Romanian intelligence advisor assigned to the PLO headquarters in Beirut reported that Arafat and his KGB handlers were preparing a PLO commando team headed by Arafat's top deputy, Abu Jihad, to take American diplomats hostage in Khartoum, Sudan, and demand the release of Sirhan Sirhan, the Palestinian assassin of Robert Kennedy.

> "'St-stop th-them!' Romanian dictator Nicolae Ceaucescu yelled in his nervous stutter, when I reported the news. He had turned as white as a sheet.

Just six months earlier Arafat's liaison officer for Romania, Ali Hassan Salameh, had led the PLO commando team that took the Israeli athletes hostage at the Munich Olympic Games, and Ceaucescu had become deathly afraid that his name might be implicated in that awful crime.

"It was already too late to stop the Abu Jihad commandos. After a couple of hours we learned that they had seized the participants at a diplomatic reception organized by the Saudi embassy in Khartoum and were asking for Sirhan's release. On March 2, 1973, after President Nixon refused the terrorists' demand, the PLO commandos executed three of their hostages: American Ambassador Cleo A. Noel Jr., his deputy George Curtis Moore, and Belgian *charge d'affaires* Guy Eid.

"In May 1973, during a private dinner with Ceaucescu, Arafat excitedly bragged about his Khartoum operation. 'Be careful,' Ion Gheorghe Maurer, a Western-educated lawyer who had just retired as Romanian prime minister, told him. 'No matter how high-up you are, you can still be convicted for killing and stealing.'

"'Who, me? I never had anything to do with that operation,' Arafat said, winking mischievously.

"In January 1978, the PLO representative in London was assassinated at his office. Soon after that, convincing pieces of evidence started to come to light showing that the crime was committed by infamous terrorist Abu Nidal, who had recently broken with Arafat and built his own organization.

"'That wasn't a Nidal operation, it was ours,' I was told by Salameh, Arafat's liaison officer for Romania. Even Ceaucescu's adviser to Arafat, who was well familiar with his craftiness, was taken by surprise. 'Why kill your own people?' Col. Constantin Olcescu asked.

"'We want to mount some spectacular operations against the PLO, making it look as if they had been organized by Palestinian extremist groups that accuse the chairman of becoming too conciliatory and moderate,' Salameh explained. According to him, Arafat even asked the PLO Executive Committee to sentence Abu Nidal to death for assassinating the PLO representative in London."

Arafat has made a political career by pretending that he has not been involved in his own terrorist acts. But evidence against him grows by the day. James Welsh, a former intelligence analyst for the National Security Agency, has told a number of US journalists that the NSA had secretly intercepted the radio communications between Yasser Arafat and Abu Jihad during the PLO operation against the Saudi embassy in Khartoum, including Arafat's order to kill Ambassador Noel. The conversation was allegedly recorded by Mike Hargreaves, an NSA officer stationed in Cyprus, and the transcripts were kept in a file code-named "Fedayeen."

For over thirty years the US government has considered Arafat a key to achieving peace in the Middle East. But for over twenty years Washington also believed that Ceaucescu was the only communist ruler who could open a breach in the Iron Curtain. During the Cold War era, two American presidents went to Bucharest to pay him tribute. In November 1989, when the Romanian Communist Party reelected Ceaucescu, he was congratulated by the United States. Three weeks later he was accused of genocide and was executed, dying as a symbol of communist tyranny.

It is high time that the US end the Arafat fetish as well. President Bush's current war on international terrorism provides an excellent opportunity.

Arafat's Harvest of Hate, by Charles Krauthammer, reprinted in the *Jerusalem Post*:

> "September 11 awakened Americans to the anti-American vitriol in the state-controlled media of such apparently friendly states as Egypt and Saudi Arabia. We are just beginning to understand how a daily diet of hatred fed through schools and the media found its most perfect expression in the slaughter of September 11.

> "We have failed, however, to see how a similar campaign of hate has laid the groundwork for the orgy of murder-suicide the Palestinians are now engaged in. A mother appears on a videotape proudly sending her eighteen year-old to his death just so he can kill as many Jews as possible. This is unprecedented. Before the Oslo peace accords of 1993 suicide bombing was a practice almost unheard of among Palestinians.

> "And it is not as if they had no grievances before 1993. The advent of suicide bombings coincides precisely

with the era of Israeli conciliation and peacemaking: recognition of the PLO, repeated concessions of territory, establishment of the Palestinian authority, acceptance of an armed Palestinian police – all culminating in the unprecedented offer of an independent Palestinian state with its capital in a shared Jerusalem. It is precisely in the context of the most accommodating, most conciliatory, most dovish Israel policy in history that suicide bombing took hold.

"Where then did they come from? During the last eight years, the years of the Oslo 'peace process,' PA Chairman Yasser Arafat had complete control of all the organs of Palestinian education and propaganda. It takes an unspeakable hatred for people to send their children to commit Columbian-like murder-suicide. Arafat taught it. His television, his newspapers, his clerics have inculcated an anti-Semitism unmatched in virulence since Nazi-Germany.

"When US peace negotiator Dennis Ross stepped down last year, he acknowledged, to his credit, that a major error of diplomacy in the Clinton years was turning a diplomatic blind eye to the poisonous incitement in Palestinian media. Just as Osama bin Laden spent the 90s indoctrinating and infiltrating in preparation for murder, Arafat raised an entire generation schooled in hatred of the 'Judo-Nazis.' This indoctrination goes far beyond expunging Israel, literally, from Palestinian maps. It goes far beyond denying, indeed ridiculing, the Holocaust as a Jewish fantasy. It consists of the rawest incitement to murder, as in this sermon by Arafat-appointed and Arafat-funded Ahmad Abu Halabiya broadcast live on official PA television early in the intifada. The subject is 'the Jews' (Note, not the Israelis but the Jews.):

"They must be butchered and killed as Allah the Almighty said: Fight them. Allah will torture them at your hands. Have no mercy on the Jews, no matter where they are, in any country. Fight them wherever you are. Wherever you meet them, kill them.'

"The rationale offered for such murder is Jewish villainy as taught not just in Palestine but throughout the Arab world. On March 10, for example, an article in the official Saudi newspaper, *al Riyadh,* described in rich detail how the Jews ritually slaughter Christian and Moslem children to use their blood in their holiday foods. With almost comic Saudi pseudo-scholarship, it explained that for one holiday (Purim) the Jews must kill an adolescent, but for Passover the child must be ten years or younger.

"When the article achieved wide notoriety in translation, the editor apologized under pressure. He said he had been out of town when the article appeared. An odd excuse, given the fact that this elaborate blood libel ran as a two-part series.

"A precondition for peace is to prepare your people for peace. Egypt's Anwar Sadat did that after signing his peace treaty with Israel. The Israelis did that after signing Oslo. They changed their textbooks and altered their civic culture to recognize and accept the Palestinians. On the fiftieth anniversary of Israel's independence, for example, Israeli television aired an epic multi-part historical documentary that offered a view of the Palestinians that was deeply sympathetic and understanding.

"While Israeli leaders, both political and intellectual, were preparing their people for peace, Arafat was preparing his people for war – the war he unleashed two months after rejecting Israeli's Camp David peace offer of July 2000 – with an unrelenting campaign of anti-Semitic vilification carried out by every organ of his media. And how he succeeded. When Arafat's state-controlled media glorify a 'martyrdom operation' it is not just a commendation of murder, it is a vindication of their own pedagogy. We now see its fruits in the streets of Jerusalem, where the blood from the latest suicide bombing graces the third floor of surrounding buildings."

Under the title *EU and the PA*, David M. Weinberg wrote in the *Jerusalem Post* on August 25, 2002:

"The European Union continues to pour oodles of aid money into the economically and politically corrupt Palestinian Authority. Less known is the fact that liberal amounts of these funds serve to promote the most extreme Palestinian aspirations and political goals, including the right of return.

"EU External Affairs Commissioner Chris Patten would have us believe that EU assistance to the Palestinians is mainly humanitarian; that it is carefully monitored; and that it is a lever for reform. In a letter published in this paper on July 18, Patten added that 'the EU has no reason to be ashamed at its efforts to maintain the PA as a valid interlocutor for Israel, in order to prevent a slide into even greater chaos and anarchy.'

"I am glad that Patten believes his own platitudes. After all, Patten is behind the 1.4 billion euros that the EU has dished out to Palestinians since 1994, not including about one billion euros more that has been contributed directly by various European states. In fact the EU has provided about a quarter of all international assistance to the Palestinians over the past eight years, according to a study to be published this fall by Dr. Gil Feiler of the Begin-Sadat Center for Strategic Studies."

However, if you open up the EU aid books – some of the information is available on the web site of the EU Delegation in Tel Aviv – a different picture emerges.

"To begin with, only half of the annual aid to the Palestinians is allocated for 'humanitarian purposes.' This includes assistance to the PA, to Palestinian NGOs, and to UNWRA for emergency food aid, post injury rehabilitation, psycho-social support, health services, cash assistance to 'special hardship cases,' water, electricity, shelter, non-food humanitarian items, environmental services, education, infrastructure, interest subsidies for the private sector, etc.

"I have no problem with this, despite the fact that the EU has never provided similar assistance to innocent, terrorized, and traumatized Israeli citizens who also could use help in post injury rehabilitation, psychosocial support, cash assistance to special hardship cases, and so on. The EU is entitled, after all, to help one side of the conflict more than the other.

"The real problem starts with the other half of EU aid to the Palestinians, monies allocated to sustaining the PA, Israel's 'valid interlocutor' according to Patten. Forty-five percent of EU aid is devoted to covering the salaries of the PA's bloated municipal, social, and security bureaucracies. Indeed, two thirds of the PA's 90 million euro monthly budget is devoted to salaries. Ten percent of this budget (about 9 million euros) is transferred monthly by the EU. This bloated bureaucracy is the mainstay of Arafat's regime: a corrupt, violent regime. It is a regime unwilling to compromise with Israel but willing to cooperate with Hamas and Jihad; a regime that boasts the largest 'police force' per capita in the world (for which the EU is paying) but nevertheless unwilling to stop terrorism against Israelis. By propping up the present PA regime, Chris Patten's EU is prolonging chaos and anarchy, not preventing it.

"Even more infuriating is the fact that Patten's aid administrators willfully ignore the corruption. According to documents captured by the IDF during Operation Defensive Shield, the PA deploys a crafty double-reporting system to skim off funds for non-salary purposes (meaning terrorism) totaling as much as 40 percent of the 60 million it gets from international donors for the payment of salaries.

"The PA's cunning works like this: it overreports its real salary needs by one third and it manipulates exchange rates in order to manufacture unreported surpluses by delaying payment to its employees. It even pads the employee rolls with hundreds of Fatah activists, and it deducts one to two percent from the salaries of security forces' personnel as 'Fatah membership fees.' These fees are then used to finance local militias and direct terrorist activities, according to the unassailable documents captured by the IDF.

"It gets worse. About 5 percent of the EU funding for the Palestinians are devoted, ostensibly, to the 'promotion of peace.' These funds have been allocated, however, mainly to organizations that scorn, not promote, Mid East peace; groups that encourage, not curb, radical Palestinian demand and goals.

"Under the rubric of the MEDA, Democracy Promotion and People to People – Permanent Issues Programs, the EU lavishes funds on the most viciously anti-Israel 'human rights' groups, including Al Haq, Law, Adala, and other 'promoters of democracy' (over 500,000 euros for 2000, and apparently in 2001 and 2002 as well.)

"The Israeli Committee Against House Demolitions received 250,000 euros, as did Ir Shalem, which seeks to 'block Jewish development of sites in the Moslem Quarter, Har Homah, Ras el Amud, Silvan, near Orient House,' etc. The EU also finances the 'monitoring of Israeli colonizing activities' to the tune of 500,000 euros.

"Sharing this largesse, strangely, was the Four Mother's Movement to Leave Lebanon in Peace (allocated 250,000 euros in 2002, which was 100 percent of its total budget). Somehow, the glorious Four Mothers do not strike me as key contributors to Palestinian civil society or to Mid East dialogue. The support they received from the EU, rather, is a striking illustration of the EU's galling interference in Israeli politics.

"As for actual Israeli-Palestinian dialogue, alas, cut short by Arafat's war in fall 2000, the EU prefers programs run by the very extreme, hard Left in Israel, such as Peace Now, awarded 400,000 euros, and Oslo architect Prof. Yair Hirschfeld (another 400,000 euros).

"Ghassan Khatib's Jerusalem Media Communication Center, the PA's main propaganda conduit to foreign journalists, is sumptuously endowed 700,000 euros.

"My favorite EU grantee is an outfit called Middle East Center for Legal and Economic Research, which received 300,000 euro 'to identify and appraise

Palestinian refugee real estate holdings in Israel.' This clearly encourages Palestinian dreams of 'returning' to Israel; or at the very least it is designed to help the Palestinians' demand 'compensation' from Israel.

Under the title *The Moral Blindness of Terje Roed-Larsen* in the *Jerusalem Post*, August 24, 2002, leftist Hebrew University professor Shlomo Avineri writes:

"On the ninth anniversary of the conclusion of the 1993 PLO-Israel talks in Oslo, one of the Norwegian diplomats who was crucial in negotiating the agreements, Terje Roed-Larsen, published an article recalling the negotiations and hoping that an international context could be found for continuing the Oslo process ('This Time The World Has To Act,' *International Herald Tribune,* August 20*).*

"Roed-Larsen is a seasoned diplomat, steeped in the humanitarian social-democratic Norwegian tradition. He is also the UN Secretary-General's special envoy to the Middle East and has been embroiled in some of the controversies surrounding what happened during the Israeli operation in Jenin refugee camp. As a UN employee, he has to use careful language, yet his memoir, and plea for action, are examples of the hypocrisy, moral blindness, and a false even-handedness that has marred so much recent UN and EU efforts at peace-making in the Middle East.

"Larsen recalls with some understandable nostalgia the atmosphere of hope, if not euphoria, that surrounded the successful completion of the talks at Oslo. It did indeed appear at that time that the Middle East was on the verge of a new age. Yet he never confronts the causes for the failure and debacle of what was obviously one of the noblest yet deeply flawed attempts at reconciliation.

"Nowhere in his article does he mention that when all is said and done, it was Arafat's refusal at Camp David, and later at Taba, to accept the Clinton-Barak proposals, that doomed Oslo. For those who have forgotten: had Arafat accepted these proposals he would have come back from the negotiations as president of an internationally recognized Palestinian state, with around 95 percent of the territories reverting to Palestinian control, with dozens of Israeli settlements dismantled, and with Jerusalem redivided with its Arab part the capital of an independent state of Palestine.

"None of this is mentioned by Larsen, and a man from Mars landing here would have never learned from him that there has indeed been negotiating about final-status arrangements, and that the Palestinians decided once again to say 'no.' Indeed, all that Larsen has to say about why Oslo failed is that both sides 'deviated' from the Oslo principles; to wit, 'Israel expanded the occupation, and built new settlements, while Palestinian groups resorted to terror.' Such sanitized language is not only falsification of the historical record but also assumes a moral equivalence between new settlements and suicide bombings. This stinks. I have no other, more diplomatic, words for it. This is also the language of Arab propaganda, and Larsen appears to give it further currency.

"So that there should be no mistake: I am against Jewish settlements in the territories; I strongly feel that setting them up was a major mistake; and I am ready for dismantling settlements as part of a real peace package. But anyone who compares settlement activities to suicide bombings targeting civilians is a moral cripple.

"One can understand the moral sensibilities of a person of Larsen's stature for the plight of the Palestinians, and there are a lot of issues on which Israel can be criticized. But by making this comparison, Larsen reminds me of those pacifists of the 1930s, moral examples, all of them, who called for understanding the German claim to the Sudetenland in 1938 on the grounds that Hitler was, after all only calling for the right of the Sudeten-Germans for self-determination. The moral blindness of Larsen can only sadden those in Israel who are ready for true compromise with the Palestinians and are willing to pay the political and strategic price for it. Statements like these, coming from an official UN representative, only explain why the UN has until now failed to achieve anything meaningful in the Middle East, and will continue to fail if people like Larsen continue to be its spokesmen in the region.

"And I hope one day Larsen will also understand why his statements only make peace efforts more difficult. Maybe one day he may even feel ashamed for what he has just written."

Evelyn Gordon, in the *Jerusalem Post* on August 27, 2002, under the title *Roed-Larsen's Novel Yardstick*:

"I have often wondered how, after two years of terrorist warfare, people could still believe in the Oslo process. But last week, Terje Roed-Larsen finally explained it for me: all you have to do is lie about the facts. After that the desired conclusions fall into place like magic.

"Roed-Larsen, the UN's Middle East envoy and a key player in the secret talks that produced Oslo, demonstrated his technique in an article published in the *International Herald Tribune* last Tuesday. 'The principles and tactics of Oslo were the right choice nine years ago,' he wrote. 'They brought violence down to unprecedented levels, a uniform rise in Palestinian living conditions, and a balanced Palestinian budget without donor support.'

"Had Oslo actually done those things, it would indeed have been a success. Yet, in fact, even before the intifada began in October 2000, not one of those statements was true.

"First, even excluding the current violence, the Oslo Accords raised terrorism to levels unprecedented in Israel's history. Within two and a half years after Oslo was signed in 1993, Palestinian terror had claimed as many victims as it had during the entire preceding decade, which included the period of the first intifada. By five years after the accords were signed, the terrorists' death toll had surpassed that of the twelve worst years of the pre-Oslo period – the years of Arafat's mini-state in Lebanon, 1970-82, which claimed hundred and sixty-two victims and such spectacular attacks as the Munich and Ma'alot massacres. It is difficult to imagine how Roed-Larsen can interpret these statistics as a *drop* in the violence, unless dead Israelis do not figure in his tally.

"The rise in Palestinian living conditions is equally fictitious. According to World Bank estimates, per-capita gross domestic product in the West Bank and Gaza fell by an average of two to three percent per year (gains in some years offset by sharp drops in others) from the inception of the PA in 1994 to 1999 (the eve of the current war after which the decline became a nosedive). In absolute terms, GDP per-capita in the West Bank fell from almost 3,000 dollars in 1993 to 2,000 on the eve of the current intifada. And unemployment, which was generally under 5 percent in the 1980s, rose to a peak of 24 percent in 1996 before declining to a mere 12 percent or 14 percent in 1999 (depending whether you prefer World Bank or UN figures).

"As for Roed-Larsen's 'balanced Palestinian budget without donor support,' donor support for the PA actually totaled a whopping 482 million dollars in 1999, or 161 dollars per Palestinian. As Patrick Clawson recently observed in these pages, this is a level of per-capita aid virtually unmatched in the world: in recent years only Bosnia, at 185 dollars per-capita in 2002, has exceeded it.

"Finally, there is Roed-Larsen's astonishing conclusion that the current war 'came not because of Oslo but despite it. The violence and misery we are facing now are the opposite of Oslo's principles, from which both parties deviated.'

"It was the Oslo Agreements that put an unregenerate terrorist in charge of the PA and gave the Palestinian 'police' fifty thousand Kalashnikov assault rifles that have since been used to murder Israeli civilians. It further created the 'safe havens' of the PA where terrorist groups could arm, train, recruit, and generally flourish undisturbed. It even provided the PA 4 billion dollars in aid over the last eight years with no controls to prevent some of the money from being siphoned off to purchase additional arms.

"Perhaps most importantly, it was the Oslo logic that insisted that all the early evidence of bad faith – the sharp upswing in terror, the Palestinian incitement in mosques, schools and the media – be ignored rather than confronted before it exploded into the current violence. Yet, even if one discounts all these facts, Roed-Larsen's statement still posits a novel yardstick for measuring the success of a peace agreement. No longer should an agreement be judged by whether it actually brought peace; it should instead be judged by whether it might have brought peace had one side not violated it by launching a war!

"Roed-Larsen has undoubtedly done the world a valuable service by exposing the rotten foundations on which support for Oslo rests. But it is to be hoped that other public figures will not imitate his tactics. In the long run, facts are always better than lies as a basis for policy."

Reporter Tovah Lazaroff of the *Jerusalem Post* reported on August 21, 2002:

"Swedish television has apologized for airing a show earlier this month in which Jews were accused of profiting from the Holocaust and were linked to the September 11 attack on the World Trade Center in New York. The controversy over the segment was reported in a number of Swedish papers.

"'We do regret what was said,' said Swedish television communications director, Helga Baagoe. 'To say it was in bad taste is not strong enough.'

"Lisa Abramowicz, a board member of Stockholm's Jewish community, said that although the show *Trede Makten* (Third Power), which airs on Wednesday nights, is satirical, that segment crossed the line into anti-Semitism. Abramowicz said statements made by the station to date do not show that it understands the full extent of the damage done by publicizing such untruthful and inciting statements. And there have been other anti-Semitic incidents in the Swedish media."

According to a transcript she provided, the segment, narrated by a goldfish, talks about the Holocaust. 'After all, this persecution did come up trumps – it gave the Jews their own land. It is not always a bad thing to be the victim of persecution.'

> "The narrator continues, 'And the German State and the Swiss banks have had to pay financial compensation amounting to hundreds of billions of dollars.... Let's face it: The Jews have never in their history have been stronger than they are today. Incidentally, did you know that this fund was officially created in New York and was to be inaugurated in conjunction with the World Jewish Congress on the 11th of September 2001?' And then the screen showed a picture of the attack on the World Trade Center.

> "'It was shocking,' Abramowicz said. 'There was no such fund created on September 11, and even if there were, what relevance would it have to the attack?'"

Marc Daugherty reported from Brussels on one group of members in the European Parliament who were bucking the prevalent anti-Israel trend, despite the political consequences (*Jerusalem Post*, Friday, May 31, 2002):

> "As bleak as the picture looks Israel does not stand alone within the walls of the EU Parliament. Some fifty

MEPs are now leading an energetic rear-guard political action against the anti-Israel tide in Europe's legislative body. They hail from various states and hold different political views, most are non-Jewish and all are standing up for Israel despite the risk of significant personal cost to their political careers.

"Over the past month, many Israelis and supporters of Israel have questioned why, even given Europe's large Moslem population and dependence on Arab oil, the EU has taken such a tough, unsympathetic line in dealing with a democratic state faced by the constant threat of suicide bombers.

"Italian MEP Marco Panella, veteran chairman of the Radicals: 'Israel maybe represents 0.2 percent of the Middle East's surface area, yet Arab states look upon Israel as some sort of cancerous spot over their skin. They think it's melanoma, when in reality it's the threat of democracy.'"

In short, while the Oslo Accords have proven spectacularly damaging to peace in the Middle East, the general trend in Europe is, amazingly, to adhere to the Accords and to blame Israel for their failure.

CHAPTER EIGHT

The United Nations

On November 12, 1948, the General Assembly of the UN decreed that refugees who want to return to their homes and are interested in living in peace with their neighbors should be allowed to do so at the earliest possible date.

This resolution, with the full support of the nations of Western Europe, did not give any credence to the danger that these refugees would impose on a country that only recently had overcome a war of life and death. These refugees were the ones who had attempted to eliminate the newborn state. At no point did Europe take into consideration the Jewish refugees forced to leave their home countries.

Arthur L. Goodheart, in his book *D'Agression*, furnishes us with some interesting figures on Jewish and Palestinian refugees. While claims today put the number of Arab refugees at four million, in 1948 they numbered just three hundred and sixty thousand, according to UN mediator Count Bernadotte: three thousand in Iraq (in spite of Iraq's lack of manpower it refused to accept more), fifty thousand in Lebanon, seventy thousand in Syria, fifty thousand in Jordan, twelve thousand in

Egypt, one hundred and forty-five thousand dispersed in different parts of Palestine, and thirty thousand dispersed in other parts of the world.

To compare, we read in Kent Lindsay's article in *Contemporary Review* of 1946, about the number of Jews in Arab lands who escaped, or left, immigrating to Israel. [Figures show total number of Jews and (how many remained by 1960)]: twenty-six thousand (nine thousand in 1960) in Syria and Lebanon; one hundred and twenty-six thousand (six thousand) in Iraq; forty-five thousand in Yemen (three thousand and five hundred); seventy-five thousand in Egypt (seven thousand); two hundred and ten thousand in North Africa (thirty-five thousand): A total of four hundred and eighty-five thousand of whom fifty-eight thousand were still in their native countries by 1960.

There is in fact no big difference between the *numbers* of Jewish and Arab refugees. Rather, the meaningful difference is that the Jewish refugees were all absorbed and their status ceased to be that of refugees. Contrarily, the leaders of the Arab countries call their refugees "our brethren" but refuse to absorb them and let them rot in poverty.

Ovadia Sofer, in the *Jerusalem Post*, November 2001:

> "The persecution of Jews in Arab countries, which intensified after the establishment of the State of Israel, forced more than six hundred and fifty thousand Jews to abandon their homes and property in Arab countries. Palestinian refugees, numbering the same as the Jewish refugees, left Israel after the War of Independence. According to research recently published in Israel, just property confiscated by the Iraqi

authorities from its Jews totaled more than two billion dollars in 1951 prices, at the same time of massive emigration of Iraqi Jews. The State of Israel never encouraged the orderly recording of Jewish property left in Arab countries. However, there is no doubt that this property exceeds in value that abandoned by the Palestinians.

"Western TV screens are full of pictures of the poverty in Palestinian refugee camps. They ignore the fact that after World War II the number of refugees throughout the world was estimated at fifty million, forty-nine million of whom were absorbed in other countries to which they emigrated, and nothing more was heard about them. Only the Palestinian refugees have been held as hostages by their Arab brethren, under terrible conditions, despite the tremendous sums of money generously allocated to them by the international community.

"If this money had been invested in absorption of the refugees in the neighboring Arab countries, these same refugees and their descendents born in the camps, who now form a majority, would have become active contributors to the economy of the Arab countries, instead of becoming easy prey for recruitment to the ranks of the suicide bombers of Islamic terrorism. The younger generation, in not a few Arab countries, is also frustrated because of the concentration of resources of wealth in these countries in the hands of authoritarian rulers. Some of these rulers choose to allocate generous sums to terrorist organizations, whether to advance political aims, as in the case of Syria or Libya, or in order to remain in power, such as the Saudi regime that generously allocates money to all the known terrorist organizations in the Arab world.

"Palestinian terrorism was the origin, and set an example to be copied, of all the forms of terrorism currently evident in the world. Israel is frequently criticized and condemned for 'disproportionate responses' to Palestinian terrorist attacks. Unfounded accusations of this kind can be related to the biased and hostile attitude of UN institutions to the Arab-Israeli dispute. Of the hundred and ninety-five resolutions passed by the UN Security Council before 1990, ninty-seven were directed against Israel. During the same period the UN General Assembly passed four hundred and twenty-nine resolutions against Israel out of a total of six hundred and ninety.

"This biased attitude, or the attempt to balance criticism practiced by the Western leaders, some of whom are regarded as the patrons of the Palestinians, merely encourages Arafat to continue terrorism.

"If a forceful and unambiguous demand by Western European were presented to Arafat, accompanied by a warning that Europe would stop opening its leaders' doors to him, it is probable that he would change his tortuous path and make real efforts to halt the terrorism, without which peace will not come to our region."

The UN Security Council has served as little more than a platform for the Arab States to demonize and vilify the Jewish State. As an indication of the formulation of the Council's resolutions, one can observe how far the UN has strayed from the lofty principles it claims to uphold. UN partiality has been all the more glaring in light of the ongoing Palestinian terror campaign against Israel. When IDF troops entered Palestinian-controlled areas during Operation Defensive Shield, UN Secretary General Kofi Annan publicly berated the Jewish State for having the audacity to defend itself, saying, "The whole world is demanding that Israel withdraw; I don't think the whole world can be wrong." Annan's special Middle East envoy, Terje Roed-Larsen, went even further than his boss, arrogantly asserting, after IDF units entered Jenin, that "Israel has lost all moral ground in this conflict."

The UN has yet to take a firm and unambiguous stand against Palestinian terrorism. So much alacrity has been shown when Palestinians carry out attacks in the heart of Israel or massacre innocent civilians. Moreover the UN is actively involved in funding many of the hothouses of hatred and incitement run by the PA; the UNRWA is actively involved in assisting and supporting refugee camps throughout the territories, many of which have served as launching pads for terror attacks against Israel.

This biased attitude, or the attempt to balance criticism practiced by the Western leaders – some of whom should be regarded as patrons of Palestinians – merely encourages Arafat to continue terrorism. In order for Israel to abide by UN resolutions, Israel must cease to exist. A call for Israel to heed UN resolutions is a call for Israel to commit suicide.

Over the past year alone, the UN passed resolution after resolution, in the Security Council, in the General Assembly, in its Human Rights Commission, and even in its Commission on Aging, that deny Israel its legal right, under Article 51 of the UN Charter, to defend itself against aggression. In one month between March and April, the UN Security Council held thirty-two separate debates on Israel. The UN Conference on Racism last September effectively reinstated the General Assembly's definition of Zionism as Racism and thus denied that Israel has the legal right to exist under international law. In April the UN Human Rights Commission passed a resolution endorsing Palestinian terrorism against Israel.

For the past fifty-four years, the UN has followed a consistent and coherent policy regarding only one issue – anti-Semitism. Its policy had been to advance anti-Semitism by systematically and illegally discriminating against the Jewish State all the time and everywhere. In so doing, the UN has lost even the semblance of legitimacy as a world government. It cannot be regarded as a body responsible for enforcing international law, because in its systematic discrimination against Israel, it stands in breach of international law as embodied in its own charter's determination that all member states are to be treated equally.

The Durban Conference

The ostensibly anti-racist venue was abused to spread anti-Israel propaganda and anti-Semitism.

Although the US government had the fortitude to boycott this travesty, and Canada belatedly denounced the abuses, the presence and active participation of representatives from Europe and other countries provided the façade of legitimacy to racism. The wealthy and powerful non-governmental organizations that participated in Durban, such as Human Rights Watch, Amnesty International, and Oxfam, were also active in their role in promoting the hatred and incitement that is used to justify terrorism. Similarly, the outgoing Human Rights Commissioner, Mary Robinson, will be remembered primarily for her contribution to the fiasco at Durban. The Durban conference was a debacle.

The Durban theme of racism lent itself more readily to politicization, and the protocols and declarations were prepared at the preliminary meetings at Teheran.

The Geneva Convention

The US, Israel and Australia boycotted the meeting of the High Contracting Parties of the Fourth Geneva Convention to discuss the situation in the territories, with Israel saying this is a gross politicization of the Geneva Convention and yet another instrument with which to bash Israel.

"We think this is a futile exercise," said Mordechai Yedid, Israel's Foreign Ministry's deputy director-general for the UN and international organizations, noting that it came just days after a wave of terror that killed and wounded dozens of Israelis. "The draft resolution makes no reference to the Palestinians' strategic decision to engage in terrorism after Camp David, the thousands of terrorists incidents, or the over two hundred Israeli civilians who have lost their lives as a result," he said.

Israel asked the Swiss government, which convenes the conference, to cancel the meeting in Geneva, or at least to postpone it, but the call was not heeded. Consequently Israel lobbied a number of countries to either boycott the conference, or to vote against the resolutions, to no avail. Following repeated requests by Moslem states to reconvene the conference, the Swiss government opted to hold informal consultations with a number of countries and came up with a declaration that was read after the half-day conference.

While ignoring Palestinian acts of terrorism, the declaration calls upon "the occupying power to immediately refrain from committing grave breaches involving any of the acts mentioned in Article 147 of the Fourth Geneva Convention, such as willful killing, torture, unlawful deportation, willful depriving of fair and regular trial, extensive destruction, and appropriation of property not justified by military necessity and carried out unlawfully and wantonly." According to the statement, the parties to the Geneva Convention "see the need to recall basic humanitarian rules, including the prohibition at any time and in any place whatsoever on acts of violence to life and person, torture, outrages upon personal dignity and of arbitrary or extra-judicial executions."

CHAPTER NINE

The Vatican

D avid Hornik, reviewing the book *The Popes Against the Jews: The Vatican's Role in the Rise of Modern Anti Semitism* by David Kertzer, in the *Jerusalem Post*:

> "We fight the Jews not of any caste, or personal hatred, but rather because they are vampires of humanity, monopolizers, usurers, speculators; they are dishonest, implacable, destroyers and slanderers, exploiters of Christian blood.' These are the words that were published in 1892 in the Vatican's daily newspaper *L'Osservatore Cattolico*. The statement was not aberrant but in fact typical, even routine. Nor did matters improve; the Catholic Church continued to play a major role in fomenting European anti-Semitism up to the Holocaust.

> "The bleak story of the Church's anti-Semitism from the beginnings of Jewish emancipation in the early 19th century up to the outbreak of World War II is told in this book by David I. Kertzer, an author and expert

in Italian history. In the late 1990s Kertzer was one of the first scholars to be given access to long-sealed Vatican archives. The result is The Popes Against the Jews, a lucid and dispassionate account that should permanently put to rest claims that the Church was not a prime mover of modern anti-Semitism."

In 1814, according to Kertzer, after Napoleon's forces were defeated and the Italian Papal States were restored, Pope Pious VII had an opportunity to adapt the Church to the liberalization trends that were sweeping Europe, including Jewish emancipation. Instead, he denounced modernity and, concurrently, forced the Jews of the Papal States back into squalid, crowded ghettoes while reinstating such traditional practices as yellow badges, humiliating carnivals, and harsh restrictions on Jews' employment and contact with the larger Christian society.

By 1861, Italian Nationalist forces had stripped the Vatican of all political power except in Rome and its vicinity. Yet the Church, instead of making amends with modernity, continued to view itself as the beleaguered bastion of morality surrounded by pernicious trends. And at the core of these trends stood the newly liberated, malignant Jews, the 'Synagogue of Satan,' as Pope Pious IX called them in 1873, bent on the destruction of the Church and world domination.

In 1840, at the time of the infamous Damascus blood libel, the Vatican had vigorously upheld the charges in the face of liberal opinion and was outraged when the accused were finally released. But the Church did not change. Its official organs continued to focus obsessively and horrifically on ritual-murder accusations against Jews, up to and beyond the Mendel Beilis case in Kiev in 1913.

In political confrontations between liberal movements and reactionary, anti-Semitic ones, the Church always sided with the latter. Two examples: In the 1890s it backed Austria's Social Party led by the notorious anti-Semite Karl Lueger. In the Dreyfus case, the Vatican journal *Civilta Cattolica* and the Catholic press in general were in the vanguard of opposition to the falsely accused Dreyfus, and French Catholic organizations helped the 1897 anti-Semitic riots sparked by the case.

In 1918 Achille Ratti, then the reclusive, nonpolitical prefect of the Vatican library, was sent by the Vatican to Poland to report on the situation of its large Catholic population. Considering that Ratti went on to become Pope Pious IX from 1922 to 1939, Kertzer believes the solidification of his anti-Semitic attitudes during his stay in Poland had a pivotal effect on Vatican history. Jews in Poland at that time were subject to incitements and pogroms, including the Lvov pogrom in which seventy-three Jews were murdered. But the soon-to-be pope's report blamed the Jews for their own persecution, linking them with "loan sharking and contraband" and asserting that "Jewish hostility against the new state is on display everywhere."

Under the new pope in the 1920s and 1930s, the Church was the main disseminator of the *Protocols of the Elders of Zion* and other anti-Semitic works; nor did the Church raise any objection when Italian Fascists imposed anti-Semitic racial laws that were strikingly similar to traditional Church restrictions against the Jews. The Catholic establishment remained anti-Semitic up to the outbreak of the Holocaust, and the role of the subsequent Pope Pious XII during the war itself is a separate, bitterly controversial subject.

It was two events in early 1998 that led Kertzer to write this book. First, a Vatican Commission, charged by the pope with determining whether the Church bore any responsibility for the rise of modern anti-Semitism, and for the Holocaust, reported that the Catholic Church had played no role whatsoever. Second, the Vatican announced that scholars would, for the first time, be allowed into the archives of the Central Office of the Inquisition. From what Kertzer knew about the history of the Vatican relations with the Jews he was skeptical about the Commission's report and found the prospect of working in the long-sealed Inquisition's archives too exciting a possibility to pass up.

While anti-Semitism has an ancient history, the development of modern anti-Semitism, of the sort that would make the Holocaust possible, arose only in the late 19th century. The Vatican maintains that modern anti-Semitism did not grow out of the long history of Christian anti-Judaism, but from new nationalist movements that arose in Europe in the 19th century.

What Kertzer shows in his book, based largely on documents found in the Vatican archives, is that the Vatican was very much involved in the development of modern anti-Semitism.

Kertzer also shows that the distinction made by the Vatican today between religious anti-Judaism, which the Church acknowledges to have marked its past, and social, economical, political anti-Semitism, which it claims not to have embraced is not tenable.

The Vatican championed a view of Jews as sinister enemies of the state and of the people, and, well into the 20th century, called for keeping them quarantined from healthy Christian society.

Kertzer says that there are actually several different Vatican archives, and each one is a separate story. Perhaps of greatest interest from this point of view is the archive of the Inquisition.

When Cardinal Ratzinger announced that archive's opening, the *New York Times* asked Kertzer to write an op-ed about it, which he did. In order to get permission to work there, he had to send in a request directly to Cardinal Ratzinger, along with a letter of recommendation. Kertzer asked his friend, historian Carlo Ginzburg, to write for him, since when announcing the opening of the archives to scholars, the Cardinal had cited Ginzburg's request of nineteen years earlier. (The Church moves slowly!)

In January 1904 Theodor Herzl initially sought goodwill in a personal interview with Pope Pius X. The pontiff opposed the very notion of a collective return of Jews to Zion so long as they did not accept Jesus as their savior.

In May 1917 Zionist diplomat Nahum Sokolow was granted an audience with Pope Benedict XV. In contrast to his predecessor, this pontiff appeared not unsympathetic, even declaring that the return of the Jews to Palestine was a providential event that was consonant with God's will, although he insisted that a "reserved zone for the Holy Places is of extraordinary importance." Sokolow gave every insurance and the pope concluded: "Yes, yes, I do hope that we will be good neighbors." Once the Paris Peace Conference began in early 1919, Benedict XV, who had evidently had a change of heart since his talk with Nahum Sokolow two years earlier, told a secret Vatican consistory that "it would be for us and all Christians a bitter grief if the unchurched were placed in privilege and prominent position." Although the pontiff was resigned to a British mandate, he preferred that it extend no official status to the Jews. Pius XI, who succeeded Benedict in 1922, shared his predecessor's concerns. These were exacerbated when lurid reports of "Zionist Imperialism" arrived from Monsignor Luigi Barlassini, the Latin Patriarch of Jerusalem.

Throughout the 1920s and 1930s, during a period of ideological strife in Europe, papal suspicions of the Jews, inside and outside Palestine, resurfaced dramatically and invidiously. In 1929 *L'Osservatore Romano*, the official organ of the papacy, editorialized with the headline: "The Jewish Danger Threatening the Entire World." In 1936 the Jesuit paper *Civilta Catollica* insisted that "the Jews constitute a serious and permanent danger to Christianity," and a year later began publishing charges of Jewish ritual murder. A Jewish presence in the Holy Land assuredly was to be regarded as inimical to Church interests. In 1937 the Vatican urged that Jewish refugees be settled in the United States, not Palestine. When the British White Paper of 1939 foreclosed Jewish immigration to Palestine, Rome expressed its approval.

By 1939, Eugenio Pacelli had ascended the papal throne as Pius XII. His silence during the ensuing Holocaust has been extensively documented. Less well known was the implacability of his opposition to the Jewish National Home, even as an asylum for Jewish refugees. In May 1943 Luigi Cardinal Maglioni, the Vatican secretary of state, issued an explicit warning against the "Zionist enclave in the Holy Land." As late as April 1945, even with the magnitude of the Jewish tragedy more fully revealed, the Vatican would not reverse its position.

Unsettled by the declaration of Israeli independence, *L'Osservatore Romano* in May 1948 could not withhold a last, backhanded swipe at the Jews. Zionism was a military secular movement, it insisted, and Christianity alone regarded the Holy Land as integral to its very ideology. After the Arab forces invaded the Christian churches and used them as firing bases on the Israelis, and the Israeli army forced the Arabs out, the Latin Patriarch of Jerusalem accused Israel of violating "the sanctity of our churches, convents, and institutions. We therefore appeal to all those in power and to the civilized world to compel the Jews to respect the Holy Places and the religious institutions and to desist from making them into military bases and targets."

Ironically, the military division of Jerusalem between Israel and Trans-Jordan by then had become a fait accompli, one that both sides were determined to institutionalize politically. Although thirty of the thirty-four principal Christian churches and shrines in the Jerusalem-Bethlehem area had fallen under Jordanian rule, the Vatican was uninterested in exerting pressure on the Trans-Jordanian government. Year in and year out, Rome sustained a campaign not only for an internationalized Jerusalem, but for a repatriation of Palestinian Arabs to their homes, and for an Israel reduced to the frontiers envisaged in the original partition resolution.

Even more fundamentally, Israel's 1956 Sinai victory evoked a certain thoughtful reappraisal in Catholic circles. It was not irrelevant that the triumph had been achieved in conjunction with France. A significant majority within France's own Catholic hierarchy, led by Jean Cardinal Danielou, by the brave Resistance veteran Monsignor Daniel Pezer, and by Father Inges Congar, editor of *Le Croix*, the organ of progressive Catholicism in France, applauded the establishment of Israel as an act of moral justice.

The new forbearance became particularly notable during the pontificate of Angelo Roncalli. Assuming office in 1958 as John XXIII, the "good pope" reigned until 1963. As the full story emerged of Vatican passivity during the Holocaust, Rome found itself on the moral defensive. Renowned in any case for his humanity, Pope John was prepared to make overtures to the Jews, even to Israel. As early as 1959, he invested Israel's ambassador to Italy with the Grand Cross of Sylvester, a meaningful gesture after the Curia's earlier unwillingness so much as to official reference to the Jewish state. Otherwise the pontiff chose to express his goodwill by authorizing the Second Lateren Council, scheduled for 1962, to reevaluate the historic Catholic charge of deicide against the Jews. At John XXIII's instruction, a special committee under the chairmanship of Augustin Cardinal Bea, leader of the progressive element of the Vatican, worked in intimate consultation with a network of international Jewish organizations. The committee's proceedings were completed only in October 1965, two years after Pope John's death. The resulting document rejected the notion that Crucifixion could "be attributed without distinction to all Jews then alive, or to the Jews today." And thus it "deplores on religious grounds any display of anti-Jewish hatred or persecution."

In 1964 Pope Paul VI, who had succeeded John XXIII upon the latter's death the year before, embarked on a pilgrimage to Christian shrines in the Holy Land. The pontiff significantly avoided any reference to the State of Israel. In following years, contacts widened between Church leaders and Israeli officials, both in Jerusalem and Rome. Even the Vatican's tone and language toward Israel gradually softened.

On February 5, 1976, at the close of a four-day "Seminar on Islamic-Catholic Dialogue," held in Tripoli, the assembled Christian and Moslem clerics issued a joint communiqué that threatened to reopen old wounds. It endorsed the November 1975 UN General Assembly resolution equating Zionism with racism, affirmed "the national rights of the Palestinian people and their right to return to their lands," and emphasized the "Arab character of the city of Jerusalem." There could be no doubt of Vatican approbation, for the communiquÈ was promptly reported that same day in *L'Osservatore Romano*. After Israel's strong protest the next morning a Vatican statement of repudiation was duly featured in *L'Osservatore Romano*. The papacy's tactical retreat signified no fundamental change in its campaign on behalf of the Palestinian refugees.

In August 1978 Paul VI died, as did his successor, John Paul I, after an incumbency of only a few weeks. He in turn was succeeded by Karol Wojtyla – John Paul II – the first non-Italian pontiff in centuries. He evinced a characteristic papal restraint on the Arab-Israeli conflict. In March 1979, declaring his support of the impending Israeli-Egyptian peace treaty, the pope alluded only to his goodwill for all populations in the region.

With growing frequency, Israel's ambassadors to Italy were received in papal audience.

However, revived tensions between Rome and Jerusalem approached their climax with Israel's invasion of Lebanon in the summer of 1982. And then, in September 1982, following the evacuation of PLO guerrillas from Beirut, John Paul II took a step even his predecessor had not dared to do. He invited Yasser Arafat to an audience. Widely publicized, the event provoked an Israeli governmental denunciation. The September 1982 exchange was the most acrimonious in thirty-four years in Israeli-Vatican dialogue.

In December 1987 when the Palestinian intifada erupted in the West Bank, the Vatican affirmed that it maintained "serious concern about Israel's handling of Palestinian unrest." By the end of his first decade on the pontifical throne, nevertheless, the Polish Pope had moved with an equivalent forthrightness to criticize Israel's territorialism, and eventually to condemn perceived transgressions by the Jewish State against the Palestinian people. In his diplomatic odyssey through the Middle Eastern quagmire, John Paul had become a paradigm of Europe itself.

Accordingly, the Vatican daily reported in August 2002 that Israel was engaging in "aggression that turns into extermination."

AFTERWORD

A Response to the "Peace Camp"

In the past few months alone, the B'Tselem human rights group has alleged that Israel "willfully adopts the tactics of terrorists," accused IDF soldiers of being "trigger happy," and bemoaned what it termed the "IDF's loss of any compass." Its press releases, too, often parrot Palestinian propaganda.

Interestingly, however, B'Tselem and other like-minded groups have been largely silent about the PA habit of trampling the most basic of civil liberties. According to Berel Wein in the *Jerusalem Post*, August 24, 2002:

> "The Left's blaming the IDF for all imagined wrongs in our current struggle only encourages the Hamas bombers.

> "The Hague court is not going to indict Arafat ever, no matter what! They are only after us because we are not, and never have been, acceptable to European latent and overt anti-Semitic 'tastes.' The Europeans only wish to 'beautify the world,' and we are not aesthetically beautiful enough in their eyes to justify our existence as a nation, a state, or either a faith.

"The inability of the fringe Left here in Israel to give up on its outmoded, incorrect, and impractical ideology, and its continuing efforts to impose it on us once more, frightens me. The truth is that the State of Israel, the Jewish people, the laws of Torah and Jewish morality are all somehow repugnant to the tastes of our adversaries. Once again they are attempting to destroy us because we offend their aesthetic sensibilities."

Richard Bernstein in the *Jerusalem Post* on August 8, 2002:

"The day after the Palestinian attack on the Hebrew University in Jerusalem, *The Guardian*, the left-leaning English newspaper, published an editorial criticizing Israel for what the paper called 'random, vengeful acts of terror' against Palestinian civilians during its reoccupation of the West Bank town of Jenin last spring. This, after a UN report dismissed Palestinian claims that Israel had massacred civilians there.

"Over the past several months, such sentiments have become common in much of Europe. A few months ago, Tom Paulin, a poet, Oxford University professor and regular guest on BBC television, told *Al Ahram*, Egypt's leading newspaper, that American-born Jews who have settled in the Israeli-occupied West Bank were 'Nazis, who should be shot dead.' His remarks, which outraged some, were also met by approval.

"N.A. Wilson, a prominent conservative British writer and editor, publicly defended Mr. Paulin, who has also referred to Israeli soldiers as 'Zionist SS.'

"'Many in this country and throughout the world would echo his views on the tragic events in the Middle East,' said Mr. Wilson, who himself wrote in the *Evening Standard*, that he had 'reluctantly' concluded that Israel no longer had the right to exist. That, too, is a view that throughout Western Europe seems to command a fair degree of sympathy. In France, demonstrators held posters aloft saying 'death to Jews.' In Italy, *L'Osservatore Romano*, the Vatican daily, wrote that Israel was engaging in 'aggression that turns into extermination.' And José Saramago, the Portuguese noble laureate in literature, said, 'We can compare what is happening in the Palestinian territories with Auschwitz.'"

Under the title *The Challenge From Europe's Left*, Ovadia Sofer wrote in the *Jerusalem Post*:

"A look at Palestinian propaganda in Europe and the rest of the world leads to the clear conclusion that the 'new anti-Zionism,' which is just like anti-Semitism, resides within leftist and far-Left circles, and not necessarily with the extreme Right, as is commonly thought. The latter apparently choose to conceal their hatred of Jews for the time being, for tactical electoral reasons.

"Palestinian propaganda has infiltrated deep into intellectual circles and far-Left parties, exploiting their supposed sensitivity in human rights in order to harness them to the Palestinian struggle, while ignoring its negative features. The criminal terrorism

of Palestinian suicide bombers, who strike indis-
criminately at innocent women, children and the
elderly, barely gets a mumble of condemnation from
these circles. The European media calls the terrorists
'martyrs,' 'activists,' or 'militants.' These circles also
ignore the Palestinian refusal to come to terms with
Israel's existence as a Jewish State, and one of its
obvious manifestations is the Palestinian demand to
implement the right of millions of Palestinians to
return to Israel, as a condition for a peace agreement
with Israel. The intensive work of the Israeli peace
camp overseas, which fundamentally does stand
against Palestinian terrorism, has not succeeded in
mollifying criticism by the leftist European circles
against Israel. On the contrary, European leftists
usually hear the criticism voiced by the 'peace camp'
selectively, and use it to attack Israel and blindly
embrace Palestinian propaganda, which arouses
dormant anti-Semitic feelings. These are then given
expression by harassing Jewish institutions in France
and other places in Europe. No less infuriating is that
these circles, which carry the torch of defending
human rights, do not loudly condemn the killing of
innocent civilians by Palestinian suicide bombers.
This apathy is most reprehensible and inexplicable,
given that the same tactic could spread to Europe and
the Western world in general.

"The recent elections for the French presidency are a
case in point. There were no fewer than sixteen

candidates, including ten Trotskyists and other members of the far-Left. While the extreme Right, Le Pen and others, are, for the moment, avoiding addressing the Israeli issue, the far-Left candidates made their anti-Israeli vitriol part and parcel of their election campaigns. These circles are directly responsible for anti-Israeli decisions in European and international forums, including the European parliament. This phenomenon is especially salient in Scandinavian and other European countries that used to be Israel's close friends, such as the Netherlands, Denmark, and Belgium.

"An in-depth analysis of the patterns of Palestinian penetration of the European media proves there is nothing as effective as a sophisticated recruitment of influential reporters and intellectuals, as the Palestinians did by sending talented representatives to Europe's main capitals. Israel's public relations effort is facing difficult challenges we have never seen before. Israeli diplomatic delegations were and remain the most important front line position for the infiltration, contact and recruitment of a sympathetic press for Israel."

Amnon Lord, author of *The Israeli Left*, wrote about transnationalism in the *Jerusalem Post*, October 6, 2002:

"Anyone following the world press, especially the British and the European, would reach the inevitable conclusion that Israelis are the enemies of humanity.

"A transnational system is emerging based on the model of the Stalinist regime. This system needs Palestinian-Islamic terrorism against Israel to define itself, just like it needs to define the Israelis as a sort of internal enemy of the transnational regime. The non-government organizations, the human rights organizations, the UN organizations and a large part of the media are turning right before our eyes into a police system that has co-opted Palestinian terrorism and made it an integral part of itself.

"Anyone who saw Miguel Moratinus and Terje Larsen run into Yasser Arafat's arms as soon as the siege on the Mukata ended could make no mistake. They and the journalists who fell at the terrorist leader's feet are part of the transnational terror regime. Palestinian terrorism has become a whip against the Israelis, whose place in the system is equal to that of the kulaks or the bourgeois class in the revolutionary Stalinist regime. Or are the Israelis playing the old role of the Jews again?

"If we examine the emerging transnational regime we see a number of demands directed at the Israelis, with the stipulation that as long as they are not met, terrorism will go on. The justification of terrorism against Israelis by the British and European media is similar to the justification of Stalinist terrorism by Pravda and Radio Moscow. The regime defines a system of ideals and lofty values, and those who do not adjust themselves accordingly are defined as the 'enemies of the people' or 'enemies of the revolution.'

As long as all the demands of the 'human rights' organizations are not met, terrorism is justified.

"The list of demands is long: the complete decolonization of entire territories, where Jews can not own property or reside; the prohibition of any activity that gives collective expression to the Jewish religion or nationalism; doing historic justice in the form of reparations, the return of property and land of anyone who holds the key to their homes from 1948; and the canceling of the Jew's right of self defense. Anyone who thinks that Israel is only required to return territory, divide Jerusalem and return refugees is wrong. It is required to deprive any collective right and any sign of collective identity. In the state of all its citizens envisioned by professor Adi Ofir, which can be called a 'human rights state,' the army will be disbanded and in its place there will be a 'strong police force,' a phrase familiar from somewhere.

"The human rights state, like the Communist state of equality, will be a police state that will have to impose its lofty values on all of its citizens day and night, that is, on the Jews. Some of Israel's own Left attempts to apply transnationalism here by importing international elements to limit the state. The main targets of these efforts are the institutions that reflect the will of the people, such as the Knesset and the army. This influential component of the Left skillfully uses the Supreme Court against the Knesset, and the international courts against the IDF.

"Why is Israel so central to the transnational agenda? 'The dangerous nature of the Zionist organizations has increased since the establishment of the American satellite, the entity called the State of Israel. In the US the Zionists are powerfully represented among the American manipulators who plan the whole American policy of aggression. The Israeli government, which has sold itself to the American patrons, has turned Israel into a military base of American aggression. The Zionist movement and the Zionist capitalists throughout the world are one, they are tightly linked to the capitalists imperialists.'

"These sentiments can easily be found in editorials in the *Guardian* or other newspapers, or in the anti-globalist movement's clichés. They are in fact from the prosecutor's closing statement at the mock trials in Prague fifty years ago."

A Call to Europe's Politicians to Fight Anti-Semitism

Recently, Israel's Deputy Foreign Minister Michael Melchior asked European politicians to unite to fight anti-Semitism. In a meeting in the Foreign Ministry in Jerusalem with European ambassadors and representatives of the European Union, Melchior explained that anti-Semitism is not just a Jewish problem but a universal one. Such bigotry starts with the Jews but it does not end there, Melchior said, making it important for any democratic country to combat the phenomenon.

Melchior said there is a new form of anti-Semitism in which all the classical prejudices are transferred from the individual

Jew to the state. "Israel has become the Jew among the nations," he said. Such anti-Semitism harms Israel in the international arena and it is inflaming the conflict in the Middle East. "Arab anti-Semitism has become a factor which has changed our situation in the Middle East," he said.

It is one thing to have a political and territorial dispute among countries, but "unfortunately, recently the tactics have changed from a dispute over territory to a dispute over religion. Not only is Israel being delegitimized, it is being demonized," the deputy foreign minister said. "We have to fight this, because this is spreading."

This prejudice has also spread to the human rights community, with Israel singled out as if there were no other problems in any other country, Melchior said. "We have to work on the international scene, with the judicial systems, on education, and on public explanation," he added. "There are things which might seem obvious but are not obvious to people in the Middle East: that to kill people in the name of God is the worst desecration of God's name."

Melchior also spoke again of his plan to create an international non-Jewish organization based in Switzerland to fight anti-Semitism, and noted that he pays close attention to statements by EU politicians regarding the Middle East. "We are listening to the voices from Brussels. Every day we listen carefully. Also yesterday we listened carefully. We respect and assign great importance to what the European governments think of the situation here. At the same time we do not wish that this be exploited in encouraging anti-Semitism."

CONCLUSION

After a half-century of mostly lukewarm relations, the newest round of Arab aggression has been widely greeted with European indulgence and condemnation of Israel. Rather than condemn the Palestinians as war criminals for conducting massacres against Israeli civilians, the Europeans have saved their condemnations and war crimes tribunals for Israel. Rather than boycotting the Palestinian Authority, the Europeans continue financing Arafat and his henchmen, and have launched a boycott against Israel. European condemnation and hatred, the roots of European rejection of Israel, are ancient and enduring.

For the past decades Europe has played a very negative role, embracing Palestinian and Arab causes and working against Israel. Official European policy, as formed and implemented by the European Commission and the leaders of France and other countries, has been fundamentally anti-Israel and little or no credit is given to Israeli democracy, unique in the Middle East. European bureaucrats and diplomats seek to undermine Israel by channeling funds into propaganda organizations operating under the halo of human rights groups.

As a major contributor to Yasser Arafat's PA, the EU has also financed a reign of terror and corruption. Textbooks introduced by the PA and funded by Europe are responsible for spreading incitement and sustaining the hatred that has destroyed hopes for peace.

Currently, with the active help of Europe, the UN acts more as a protector of national criminality than as the enforcer of the world order as envisioned in its charter: to "reaffirm faith in fundamental human rights, in the dignity and worth of the human person, in the equal rights of men and women and of nations large or small." This language clearly articulates the principle of universality for all peoples and all nations, but facts on the ground belie this evenhandedness: Libya has been elevated to the chairmanship of the UN Commission on Human Rights; Syria is a member of the Security Council; Iraq is serving as chair of the UN's single most important disarmament negotiating forum. The EU will now welcome a one-party police state – that specializes in abduction, assassination, torture, and detention without trial – to the chair of the UN's highest body charged with defending human rights. Europe, if not quite in cahoots with gang leaders in the Middle East, is like a police force that has long ago given up imposing something close to the rule of law. Terrorism and other forms of international aggression have been allowed to rise under the rubric of "liberation struggles." Human rights have been systematically quashed in the Middle East regimes. Humane organizations are demonized by the Arab bloc and its "non-aligned" allies.

We may ask what is the deadly combination of ignorance and arrogance that has produced the failed policies in EU headquarters. Will Europe emerge as a coherent force that might be able to put some life back into a very stale and decaying structure, rejecting its policies of appeasement? Would Europe admit that support for Arafat and Palestinian terrorism was a disastrous mistake? If such a trend emerges, a fundamental correction in tone and substance of relations between Israel and the EU is possible.

Until Europe can demonstrate that it stands for something positive and coherent, its routine opposition to Israel will rightly be easy to dismiss as cynical political calculation. For Israel, the emergence of a Europe based on the combination of realism and moral backbone can mark an important step in repairing the tattered relationship.

For years, Chris Patten, External Relations Commissioner for the EU, has insisted that the PA, far from funding terror, has been a bulwark against it, and he has gone to lengths to ignore evidence to the contrary or otherwise pretend that the evidence was somehow inconclusive. According to Patten, there is, to date, no evidence to support claims that EU monies are being used to fund terrorism.

However, in February 2003, European Union parliamentarians Francois Zimeray, Armin Laschet, and their allies, garnered the one hundred and seventy-eight signatures needed to open an investigation into alleged misuses of the European Commission's funding of the Palestinian Authority. Immediately, the European anti-fraud office (OLAF) opened its own investigation in the matter. While only weeks before these developments, Patten, in response to a question by a European parliamentarian about the allegations of misuse of the funds, said he wanted an inquiry into the matter "like a hole in the head," he now tells Mr. Laschet that he "welcomes" such an inquiry.

Franz Herman Bruner, director general of the EU anti-fraud office, announced the probe, saying it follows "evaluations of information received in recent months from a number of

various sources, and related to allegations of misuse of European funds allocated to the Palestinian authority." He said OLAF had decided to set up an external investigation "on its own initiative."

If OLAF uncovers fraud or financial mismanagement, it will try to recover the money and may provide the EU or national governments with information that could lead to administrative or criminal prosecutions against individuals.

Fortunately, as with the question of PA funding, there are glimmers of a new attitude. None of this suggests that Europe has had a change of heart. But it may indicate that the Europeans are beginning to recognize that a foreign policy based on wishful thinking and moral posturing will only contribute to their continued irrelevance as serious actors on the world stage.

However, the problem is intricately involved with the deplorable attitude of the Israeli Left, some of whom, like radical Europeans, while praising the kibbutz movement or the Weizmann Institute or Israeli poets and writers, question the right to the nation's very existence. This is not a question one asks of Yemen or Iceland. Some American Jews, too, are as dangerous to Israel as certain Europeans: Henry Siegman, for example, a senior fellow on the highly influential Council on Foreign Relations, works tirelessly to promote Palestinian statehood and demonize Ariel Sharon. In his regular column in the *International Herald Tribune*, Siegman, who serves as director of International Task Force for Palestinian Institution Building, which is funded by the European Commission and by Norway, is out to "save Israel in spite of itself." Siegman is so sure that the establishment of a full-fledged, completely

independent Palestinian state is "an existential Israeli need" that he has taken to calling upon Washington "to knock some sense into the belligerents." It is hard to believe that Siegman was once executive director of the American Jewish Congress, a position he held for over twenty years. Today he spends his time championing Arafat, who has been, he thinks, unfairly "demonized" by Ehud Barak and Sharon. In Siegman's eyes, Sharon is the root of all Mid East evil. The apparent dangers of Palestinian statehood have never been considered by Siegman in any of his IHT pieces.

The Europeans are caught up in an orgy of anti-Semitism and anti-Israel feeling. However, we may hope that the Europeans will remember and realize that the demonization of the Jews before and during the Nazi regime brought about the Holocaust, not only on six million Jews who perished, but on countless millions of Europeans of every nation.